ullan,
he
door /

Teen
Mothers
and the
Revolving
Welfare
Door

In the series

Women in the Political Economy
edited by Ronnie J. Steinberg

Teen Mothers and the Revolving Welfare Door

Kathleen Mullan Harris

Foreword by

Frank F. Furstenberg, Jr.

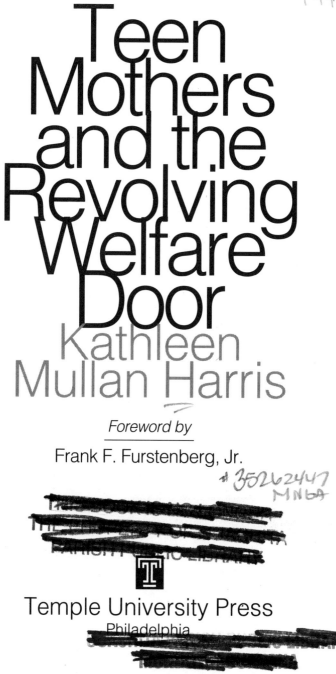

Temple University Press

Philadelphia

Temple University Press, Philadelphia 19122
Copyright © 1997 by Temple University

Published 1997

Printed in the United States of America

♾ The paper used in this publication meets the requirements of the American National
Standard for Information Sciences—Permanence of Paper for Printed Library Materials,
ANSI Z39.48–1984

Library of Congress Cataloging-in-Publication Data

Harris, Kathleen Mullan.
    Teen mothers and the revolving welfare door / Kathleen Mullan Harris; foreword
by Frank F. Furstenberg, Jr.
        p. cm. — (Women in the political economy)
    Includes bibliographical references and index.
    ISBN 1-56639-499-6 (cloth : alk. paper)
    1. Teenage mothers—United States. 2. Unmarried mothers—United States.
    3. Maternal and infant welfare—United States. 4. Child welfare—United States.
    5. Aid to families with dependent children programs—United States.
    I. Title. II. Series.
    HQ759.4.H37   1996
    306.874'3—dc20   96–36157

To my parents,
Dick and Peggie Mullan

Contents

Foreword
Frank F. Furstenberg, Jr.

This marvelously informative study about the welfare and work careers of teenage mothers is being published at a propitious moment. It is being sent to press at the very point that the system of "welfare as we know it," to borrow President Clinton's phrase, is presumably coming to an end. A near consensus that our system of public assistance is pernicious has been achieved in this country. Oddly, this consensus has been reached *without* the benefit of social science evidence—or should I say *despite* the evidence from social science research?

Americans have been persuaded by politicians, policymakers, and journalists that welfare not only is a bad idea, it has become a bad word. Even its clients and beneficiaries have learned to distrust and despise the welfare system—its bureaucracy, its rules, the stigma it brings, and its meager benefits. Little wonder that almost no one stands up for this remnant of a New Deal–era program that was never designed to serve the needs of single mothers, much less poor families (Gordon 1994). From its very inception, Aid to Families with Dependent Children (AFDC) was designed not so much to help working women who were single but to ensure that single women with young children (primarily widows when the legislation was enacted) did not have to work. A noble and perhaps even sound idea at the time, but a notion seriously outdated by social and demographic changes in the latter third of this century.

Designed to remove women from the perils of labor, the program came to be universally distrusted first because it was seen as discouraging poor women from marrying, then because it discouraged them from both marrying and working, and finally because it encouraged them to have babies in order to remain single and idle.

No one deserves more credit for selling this message to the American people than Charles Murray, whose book *Losing Ground* published in 1984 was widely heralded as a rational argument for revising welfare. Murray's argument effectively tossed the gauntlet at social scientists to disprove that welfare was *not* largely responsible for the dissolution of marriage and the rise of poverty among African Americans that occurred from the 1960s onward.

A slew of articles and books refuting Murray's use of selective and often misleading evidence and conclusions followed in the next decade. Social scientists amassed an impressive amount of data showing that Murray's argument was seriously flawed, much of it carefully reviewed by Kathleen Mullan Harris in the first chapter of this book. This evidence nicely sets the stage for the careful analysis of data on the welfare and work experiences of teenage mothers in Baltimore over a twenty-year period.

Harris exposes Murray's thesis as fallacious. The vast majority of teenage mothers treat public assistance not as a destination but as a way station to work. On occasion they cycle back onto welfare but largely because the escape routes from public assistance are uncertain. Women who leave welfare to marry, especially those with poorer education, frequently are vulnerable to returning if their marriages do not survive. Similarly, those who enter the labor force without adequate skills are especially subject to the vicissitudes of surviving in the secondary labor market—making do with low-wage jobs without security or benefits. Strategic use of welfare that leads to further education and training or to more careful marriage choices promoted autonomy in the Baltimore Study. By contrast, women who married precipitately—at the urging of their parents or "to give the baby a name"—at the cost of staying in school, had a high risk of becoming dependent on public assistance.

Harris' imaginative use of life course data to illustrate the diverse pathways that connect premature parenthood to long-term disadvantage or escape from poverty tells us that teenage mothers are no more homogeneous as a class of individuals than later childbearers. Their efforts to enter the labor force defy the stereotype that pervades current discourse about teenage parenthood, women on welfare, and single parents. Evidence from the Baltimore Study reveals the young mothers not to be calculating how to avoid responsibility for self-sufficiency but how to enter into the mainstream and remain there.

Much of what Harris reports will shore up the arguments of those who want to combine public assistance with education and job training. However, the Baltimore data tell us that it will take more than a quick fix to help many of those who are at the eye of the political storm—the chronic users of public assistance. Most of those who get stuck on welfare, pejoratively referred to as "welfare dependents" or even "addicts," are women who suffer severe deficits before they ever become pregnant. The least skilled and the most troubled, these women often remain on welfare because they have no place to go. State government can remove them from the welfare rolls but it will not help them make the transition into the labor force without intensive and extensive assistance that certainly costs more than the modest funding provided by AFDC, as we presently know it.

This study should therefore be read as solid testimony to the determination of most young mothers to attain self-sufficiency in order to support their offspring and to the difficulties that a minority are likely to face without sustained assistance. Term limits for most welfare recipients are unnecessary as they exit willingly when they have alternatives. For those lacking these alternatives, time-limited welfare is a dubious solution to an admittedly vexing problem.

The question facing those who examine Harris' findings is whether policymakers in the new era will be able to operate programs to implement what we have learned about women on welfare. To date, social science data have not played a large part in informing the public debate. Murray's rhetoric has found a more sympathetic and receptive audience than the largely contrary evidence produced by the scholarly community. The tides can change with this book which should capture the attention of policymakers with its in-depth examination and personal narratives of how young women cope with early motherhood and make decisions about family, work, and welfare.

If the new welfare system put in place is not an improvement, it will be cold comfort to the families currently on welfare for social scientists to be able to say, "We told you so." The results of this study can help inform the state policymakers who are now experimenting with varied policies and programs. If these programs are to succeed, policymakers must go beyond the public stereotypes of welfare families and become more familiar with how the poor manage their lives. If they begin with this book, they will discover that the teenage mothers in Baltimore are not really so different from the rest of us as some critics of welfare would like us to believe.

Preface and Acknowledgments

This book evolved from my research on the welfare experiences of adolescent mothers in a longitudinal study in Baltimore. One of the more important findings in that original research was the surprising amount of labor market activity that I discovered among the teenage mothers on welfare. I was surprised because the political rhetoric in the late 1980s was emphasizing nonwork as the main cause of welfare dependency, and policy solutions were therefore focused on job training and work requirements for welfare mothers to reduce welfare dependency and enforce a work ethic among the poor. Yet my research on this disadvantaged group of inner-city African-American teenage mothers indicated that many young mothers worked while they received welfare and most left welfare through work. I was puzzled that the welfare reform debates seemed to be addressing the wrong issue and that policies were being developed to require women to work when most were already working. But I had to consider the possibility that the patterns of work and welfare that I observed in the Baltimore Study were simply unique to this inner-city sample of teenage mothers, so I extended my research and carried out similar analyses with other data and studied a broader group of welfare mothers. These studies confirmed my earlier findings, and I returned to tell the story of the Baltimore mothers contained in this book.

If welfare is eliminated, how will teen mothers and their families fare? How do teen mothers use the welfare system? Are the majority long-term recipients? What are the success stories? While we have gained considerable knowledge about the welfare patterns of single mothers, we know very little about teenage mothers, the focus of current welfare policy debates. To understand how such policies might affect a substantial segment of the welfare population, we must first understand how teenage mothers use the welfare system throughout their parental life courses.

This book describes a unique longitudinal study of urban black teenage mothers and their welfare experiences during twenty years following their first birth. Most of the school-aged mothers were unmarried at the time of birth and came from very poor families, many of which were on public assistance when the adolescent first became pregnant. This study traces their subsequent life course trajectories that include work, marriage, cohabitation, subsequent childbearing, schooling, and living arrangements, and the way in which unfolding events along these trajectories intersect with their welfare trajectory. Quantitatively, I explore their patterns of welfare receipt in depth by examining the circumstances of welfare entry, the length of time of receipt, and the routes out of welfare dependency, focusing particularly on the process of leaving welfare through labor market experience. With qualitative data, I illustrate three types of welfare patterns among the teen mothers and the long-term consequences of these different economic strategies involving welfare receipt.

Although welfare touched the majority of the teen mothers' lives, the average length of receipt was short, and chronic dependence on welfare was rare. I document substantial labor market activity among teen mothers on welfare, but work does not always provide a permanent exit from welfare because most women work in low-wage jobs without employee benefits, which cannot support their families or insure their children's health. As a result, many women cycle between work and welfare over time. I therefore address the question that policy should have addressed in the late 1980s: why doesn't the work that welfare mothers do keep them off welfare? The idea that welfare recipients need work requirements in order to get them into the labor market is out of touch with the realities of welfare mothers' lives. I conclude the book by urging policymakers to pay attention to the conditions of work among welfare mothers, not the presence or absence of work effort.

When a project such as this spans a number of years and generates additional research, there are many debts that accrue: I owe much to those who have helped me along the way with their support, encouragement, intellectual exchange, and advice. I am grateful for the lifelong support of my parents, to whom I dedicate this book. In either their naivete or their brilliance, my parents led me to many doors of opportunity, never opening them for me, but letting me choose and struggle through each door on my own. I also thank my brother, Michael, who encouraged me to stay with this project to completion and who struggled through many doors with me.

For their time and wisdom, I am eternally grateful to my mentors and advisors at the University of Pennsylvania: Frank Furstenberg, who supervised my dissertation research and who remains a constant source of encouragement and support in all my professional endeavors; Phil Morgan, with whom I reached new insights into my research through lengthy discussions and who helped me set my professional sights high; and Jerry Jacobs, who initiated the process for me to write this book. I would also like to thank Ann Miller, Doug Massey, Sam Preston, and Herb Smith, for the confidence that they have displayed in me, and Paul Allison and Chuck Denk for their methodological guidance in this research. I am also grateful for the thoughtful comments and suggestions of Kristen Moore, Ronnie Steinberg, and Michael Ames.

There are a number of individuals who helped me complete this book at the Carolina Population Center at the University of North Carolina at Chapel Hill. Lynn Igoe, with the assistance of Laurie Leadbetter and Mary Jane Hill, was invaluable in hunting down and checking my abundant references. Word processing and graphics support was provided by Diana Shumaker, Amanda Quinby, and Amy Preble, and data assistance from Kim Fisher and Jeremy Marmer completed the tables. Comments and advice from my colleagues in the Sociology department—Ron Rindfuss, Guang Guo, Barbara Entwisle, and Judith Blau—helped to sharpen the manuscript. I am especially grateful to Sage Publicatons, Inc. and the *Journal of Family Issues,* 12(4), for the use of selected material and data from "Teenage Mothers and Welfare Dependency," in Chapter 7.

Finally, I acknowledge the encouragement and support of my family—Stuart, Kort, Matt, and Caitlin—who gave up their time on the web, agreed to turn down the TV and CD player, and ate a lot of spaghetti during all the years of this project.

Kathleen Mullan Harris

Teen Mothers and the Revolving Welfare Door

Chapter 1
Adolescent Mothers and Poverty

U nwed teenage mothers symbolize a stubborn and disturbing form of poverty in America. It is a poverty that many argue can be avoided by delaying childbearing (e.g., Hayes 1987; Hofferth and Moore 1979; Hoffman, Foster, and Furstenberg 1993a). It is a poverty that some feel is brought on by our social welfare system, which encourages early childbearing by offering cash assistance to women who have nonmarital births (e.g., Gilder 1981; Mead 1986; Murray 1984). It is a poverty that some feel is less deserving of public aid because it is the result of behavior that runs counter to traditional values involving marriage and family (see Whitehead 1993). And it is a poverty that may be inevitable for the women who become teen mothers, for others argue that teen childbearing is only a symptom of poverty, a legacy of growing up in an impoverished environment, with deteriorating schools and dangerous neighborhoods, and few opportunities that provide meaning and status in life (Burton 1990; Geronimus and Korenman 1992; Ladner 1971; Stack 1974).

The association between teen childbearing and poverty is unmistakable. Women who grow up in poor families begin childbearing at a younger age than nonpoor women (Abrahamse, Morrison, and Waite 1988; Duncan and Hoffman 1990b; Haveman and Wolfe 1994; Hayes 1987; Hofferth and Moore 1979; Hogan and Kitagawa 1985; Luker 1991; Michael and Tuma 1985; Plotnick 1990). Compared to women who delay childbearing beyond their teen years, women who have their first child as a teenager attain less education, work less, earn less, are more dependent on federal aid, have less support from a husband, have more children, and spend more time as a single mother (Bane and Ellwood 1983; Butler 1992; Duncan 1984; Ellwood 1986; Furstenberg,

1

Brooks-Gunn, and Morgan 1987; Hofferth and Hayes 1987; Hoffman, Foster, and Furstenberg 1993a; Marini 1984; Moore 1978; Moore and Waite 1981; Mott and Marsiglio 1985; Teti and Lamb 1989). Welfare recipients are overrepresented by single mothers who began childbearing as teenagers (Moore et al. 1987). More than half of all welfare recipients were teenagers when their first child was born (Moore and Burt 1982), and as a result, over half the AFDC (Aid to Families with Dependent Children) budget is spent on public assistance for families formed by teenage mothers (Burt 1987; U.S. House of Representatives 1993, 1148; Wertheimer and Moore 1982).[1] And perhaps most alarmingly, nonmarital teen parenthood is on the rise (see Furstenberg, Brooks-Gunn, and Morgan 1987; Hayes 1987; Hofferth and Hayes 1987; Moore and Snyder 1996).

Social and fiscal concern over early nonmarital childbearing escalated throughout the 1980s and tops the list for policy action in the 1990s. Prior to 1980 the public discourse over teenage childbearing and welfare dependency focused on alleviating the adverse consequences of nonmarital childbearing by providing mothers with economic support, education, and job training, and by fostering children's development. During the 1980s, however, attention shifted toward curbing the incidence of teenage parenting by *eliminating* economic support as an incentive for nonmarital childbearing and by enforcing work among welfare mothers. The 1990s logic centers on the notion that our well-intentioned social programs, designed to provide cash assistance to young poor single mothers so that their families would not be destitute and mothers could still stay home to nurture young children, ended up encouraging women to have children outside of marriage and discouraging work, especially among young poor mothers whose economic prospects were not very favorable anyway.

Trends in out-of-wedlock childbearing among teenagers and in the changing composition of the poverty population seem to support this logic. In 1960, 15 percent of all births to teenagers were out of wedlock. By 1993 the percentage of teenage births to unwed mothers had reached 72 percent, almost five times the 1960 level (U.S. National Center for Health Statistics 1967; Ventura et al. 1995). Among the various confounding factors affecting the trend in out-of-wedlock childbearing in the United States, the declining prevalence of early marriage has had the largest impact over time.[2] Marriage among teenagers has declined substantially since 1960, particularly for blacks, where the proportion of teenagers who were ever married dropped from 16.2 percent in 1960 to 1.4 percent in 1993 (Moore et al. 1987; Saluter 1994). As a result, the rise in nonmarital childbearing largely reflects the changing marital composition of teen mothers, not an "epidemic" of teen childbearing overall (Vinovskis 1988). From 1960 to 1993 the rates of teenage childbearing among *all teenagers* generally declined,[3] whereas the birthrate among unmarried teenagers more than doubled. Thus, the number of teenagers having babies is not increasing, but those teenagers who are having babies are increasingly unmarried.

The trends in teenage childbearing vary substantially by race. Although it was three times more likely that a black teenager would have a child outside of marriage than a white teenager in 1993, the fertility rate for unmarried white teenagers has risen more rapidly in the last twenty years—increasing by more than 200 percent, compared to an 8 percent increase among blacks (Ventura et al. 1995). Nevertheless, teenage parenthood is most often associated with the black population where practically all childbearing (93 percent) among adolescents was out of wedlock in 1993 (Ventura et al. 1995).

Coupled with the earlier rise in divorce, the increase in nonmarital childbearing resulted in an unprecedented growth in families headed by women (Garfinkel and McLanahan 1986). Between 1960 and 1993, the proportion of children under age eighteen living with a single mother increased from 8 percent to 24 percent, and these changes have had a profound effect on the well-being of American families (Saluter 1994). Most dramatic was the changing composition of the poverty population, whose faces increasingly became those of women and children. Although a little more than one in five U.S. families with children was headed by a woman in 1993, three out of five poor families with children were female headed (Rawlings 1994; U.S. Bureau of the Census 1995). Family structure now serves as a proxy for the social and economic fortunes of family members, especially children (McLanahan and Sandefur 1994). Fifty-four percent of children living in female-headed families are poor, nearly five times the 12 percent poverty rate among children living in all other families (U.S. Bureau of the Census 1995).

Of the two sources of female-headed families, never-married mothers are much poorer than their divorced counterparts (Besharov 1989; Bianchi 1993). In 1993 the median family income for never-married

3

mothers with children under eighteen was $9,292; about half the median income of divorced women with children ($17,014). As a result, two-thirds of children with a never-married mother lived in poverty in 1993, compared to 38 percent who lived with a divorced mother (Saluter 1994). Moreover, children of never-married mothers are three times more likely to be on welfare than are children of divorced mothers (Eberstadt 1988). Because marriage rates are lower and childbearing earlier in the black population (Cherlin 1992), female headship and poverty are much more prevalent among blacks than whites (Garfinkel and McLanahan 1986).

The links between race, teenage childbearing, single mothers, and poverty are rooted in the numbers, and eventually began to embody the image of a welfare recipient. Growth in the welfare population and expansion of social welfare programs and social spending coincided with the early rise in nonmarital childbearing and female headship in the late 1960s and throughout the 1970s (Burtless 1994; Danziger and Weinberg 1994). Single black mothers became the standard illustration of a growing urban underclass as reports of a breakdown of social order in the inner city that threatened to infiltrate mainstream youth in the suburbs proliferated in scientific research and the popular media (e.g., Jencks and Peterson 1991; Lemann 1986; Murray 1984; Wilson 1987). A growing segment of the population appeared to live by a different set of rules and behaviors that seriously threatened the future of the American family. The teenage mother and her fatherless children became the symbols of the underclass culture, eschewing American values of marriage and work at the expense of working Americans and the government. These images were further reinforced in the public mind by the journalistic accounts of a self-perpetuating welfare culture portrayed by the distorted worldview of inner-city youth. On camera, young men bragged about how many children they had fathered out of wedlock. Teenage girls acted as though having children outside marriage was inevitable and acceptable. And it appeared that welfare was nourishing such social disorder.[4]

The logic that welfare encourages nonmarital childbearing, especially among teenagers, seems plausible on the surface. However, a more indepth examination of the causal role of welfare in influencing the fertility behavior of teenage and unmarried women exposes the weakness of this logic.

4

Teenage Childbearing and Social Welfare in Perspective

Compared to other Western nations today, the birth rate among American teenagers is much higher. The United States has the highest rate of teenage childbearing in the industrialized world at 61 births per 1,000 teenagers, followed by the United Kingdom and Canada, whose rates are about half that of the U.S. (see fig. 1.1). In general, the European countries have far lower teenage birth rates, and Japan has the lowest rate of 4 births per 1,000 teens. The higher U.S. teenage birth rate is not due to minority teens. The birth rate among U.S. non-Hispanic whites was 42 per 1,000 teenagers in 1992, still higher than the other industrial nations (Moore, Snyder, and Glei 1995).

The international comparison provides further insight into the relationship between social welfare and nonmarital teenage childbearing. If welfare benefits provide an incentive for teenage and unmarried women to have children, then we would expect countries with higher welfare benefits to have higher rates of teenage and nonmarital fertility. The European countries have more generous social welfare benefits for single mothers than the U.S. (McFate, Lawson, and Wilson 1995), and yet their

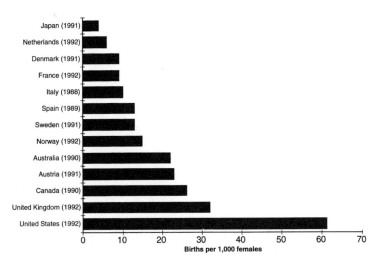

Figure 1.1 Births per 1,000 Females, Aged 15–19, for Selected Countries. (Source: Moore, Snyder, and Glei, 1995)

5

rates of teen childbearing are only one-eighth to about one-half of the U.S. rates. A country that is similar to the U.S. in many respects is Canada, whose public assistance programs for poor single mothers provide about twice as much support than in the U.S. Yet Canada's teen childbearing rate is less than half that of the U.S., and its illegitimacy rate is far below that of the United States (McFate, Lawson, and Wilson 1995).

The heightened public concern over teenage childbearing and welfare receipt in the U.S. has also led to the impression that most births outside marriage are to teenagers. Often overlooked is the fact that the increase in nonmarital fertility has occurred across all ages of women. Out of all births to unmarried women, only 30 percent are to teenagers (Ventura et al. 1995). Welfare could still operate as an incentive for unwed parenting at all ages of women; however, the increase in births among unmarried women is not limited to those who rely on welfare for support. It is a social phenomenon spread throughout the income distribution as the rise in unwed motherhood has occurred in all income and social class categories as well (Ventura et al. 1995). Since it would not make sense for a middle-class woman to give up her job and income security by having a birth outside of marriage in order to receive AFDC, the role that welfare has played in the widespread increase in nonmarital childbearing in the U.S. must be relatively minor.

An examination of the trends in nonmarital teenage childbearing and welfare benefits casts further doubt on the contention that welfare acts as an incentive to teenaged childbearing. Although welfare programs and social spending increased in the early 1970s, when the rise in unwed births first occurred, social programs have been severely cut back and welfare benefits have fallen in real value over the past twenty years, yet nonmarital teenage childbearing has continued to increase (Burtless 1994; Danziger and Weinberg 1994). In 1972 the typical woman with two children and no other income would have received $900 a month (in 1993 dollars) from AFDC and food stamps combined. In 1993 the typical woman received $658 (U.S. House of Representatives 1994). To attribute the rapid increases in unwed teenage childbearing over the last two decades to social welfare benefits doesn't make sense: the benefit levels have been declining.

Social science research has also found little support for a causal role of welfare. Most research examining the effect of higher welfare benefits on out-of-wedlock childbearing and teen pregnancy finds that benefit levels have no significant effect on the likelihood that black women and girls will have children outside of marriage and either no significant effect, or only a small effect, on the likelihood that whites will have such births (see Duncan and Hoffman 1990a; Ellwood and Bane 1985; Lundberg and Plotnick 1990; Plotnick 1990). In Robert Moffitt's (1992, 56) comprehensive review of the research on the incentive effects of the welfare system, he concludes, "The failure to find strong benefit effects is the most notable characteristic of this literature."

Although the current evidence does not indicate that welfare is a major incentive for teens to become parents, welfare is a frequent outcome of teenage childbearing. Clearly, the U.S. has a teen childbearing problem, and the subsequent poverty and welfare receipt associated with teen parenting is a pressing social concern. But public distaste for our welfare system is growing, and tolerance for supporting women who have children outside of marriage before they have reached adulthood is waning. Working middle-class families feel less generous toward the poor as they face increasing job and income insecurity themselves. Finishing school, getting a job, being able to support the children you have are American values that sustain American ideals in family and work. Unwed teenage mothers appear to have broken all the rules, and the public mood is somber. Welfare reform is focused on unwed teenage mothers and seeks to eliminate public assistance to families formed by nonmarital teenage childbearing in the hopes of discouraging future unmarried teens from becoming mothers before adulthood.

If welfare is eliminated, how will teen mothers and their families fare? How do teen mothers use the welfare system? Are the majority long-term recipients? What are the success stories? While we have gained considerable knowledge about the welfare patterns of single mothers, we know very little about teenage mothers, the focus of welfare policy debates. To understand how such policies might affect a substantial segment of the welfare population, we must first understand how teenage mothers use the welfare system throughout their parental life courses. To what extent are the welfare dynamics of teenage mothers different than those of all single mothers?

This book describes a unique longitudinal study of black teenage mothers and their welfare careers during twenty years following the birth of their first child. The data come from the Baltimore Study (Furstenberg

7

1976; Furstenberg, Brooks-Gunn, and Morgan 1987), which traced the lives of a cohort of adolescent mothers who had their first child in the late 1960s when they were eighteen years old or younger. Most of the school-age mothers were unmarried at the time of birth and came from very poor families, many of which were on public assistance when the adolescent first became pregnant. Their patterns of welfare receipt are explored in depth by examining the circumstances of welfare entry, the length of time of receipt, and the routes out of welfare dependency. This study also addresses the welfare behavior and labor market activity of the teenage mothers—the central focus of welfare reform over the last three decades. To get a flavor of the political climate in which public discourse over poverty and welfare reform has occurred, an overview of recent policy debates is presented.

The Evolution of the Contemporary Social Welfare Debate

Poverty in America reemerged as one of the leading political and social issues in the 1980s. Despite the expansive and ambitious social welfare programs implemented through the Great Society agenda of the 1960s, poverty in the United States refused to go away. The poverty rate in 1984 stood at 14.4, about the same as it was in 1966 (14.7) when the War on Poverty was launched by the Johnson administration (Danziger and Weinberg 1994). Just as the vivid accounts of hunger and deprivation in Michael Harrington's *Other America* (1962) galvanized the nation into action during the 1960s, reports of a growing subculture of isolated urban poor portrayed by ghetto blacks, teenage mothers, fatherless children, and idle youth heightened concern with poverty in the 1980s and brought social welfare into the public arena again. In 1964 one in five Americans was poor. Following the Great Society reforms to expand social welfare programs and erase poverty, still one in seven was poor in 1984. Indeed, when President Reagan began his second term in January 1985, he told the Associated Press, "In the war on poverty, poverty won" (Moynihan 1986).

The level of poverty in the United States was not stable over the past three decades, however. There was a dramatic decrease in poverty until the late 1960s, when the War on Poverty was mounted. Using the official measure, the poverty rate dropped from 19.0 in 1964 to 12.1 in 1969

(Danziger and Weinberg 1994).[5] Improvement then slowed during the decade of the seventies, at a time when federal spending on social programs for the poor was the highest. The proportion of the population falling below the official poverty line fluctuated around 11.5 for the balance of the 1970s. The poverty rate then rose sharply in the early 1980s, reaching its highest point of 15.2 in 1983. Poverty has remained stubbornly high since then. While the rates trended downward slightly to a low of 12.8 in 1989, poverty is back on the upswing in the 1990s, with 15.1 percent of the population officially poor in 1993 (U.S. Bureau of the Census 1995).

In an attempt to interpret these trends, various scholars argued their theories to explain the persistence of poverty in the 1980s and why the social policies of the 1960s fell short of their goal to eliminate poverty. As opposing perspectives emerged, the controversy resulted in a social debate over the sources of poverty and the existence of a distinct class of the welfare dependent entrapped at the bottom of American social structure. Welfare reform became a top priority of the Reagan administration as the government tried to reconcile escalating federal deficits with a social welfare system that seemed ineffective in relieving long-term poverty.

Although the 1980s controversy over social welfare surfaced in response to the apparent failure of the Great Society programs to effectively combat poverty, the debate over public support for the poor has a long social history and a familiar pattern. There has never been a time in U.S. history when our population has not contained poor individuals, but only periodically is their condition rediscovered, igniting a recurring dialogue of reform. The welfare system is attacked for what it can and cannot do to improve the plight of the poor, and advocates for reform come from both sides of the political spectrum. Michael Katz (1986) explains in his social history of welfare in America: "Nobody likes welfare. Conservatives worry that it erodes the work ethic, retards productivity, and rewards the lazy. Liberals view the American welfare system as incomplete, inadequate, and punitive. Poor people, who rely on it, find it degrading, demoralizing, and mean. None of these complaints are new; they echo nearly two centuries of criticism" (ix).

The view that social welfare programs actually harm the poor by driving them deeper into poverty is a classic conservative argument (Piven and Cloward 1971). Historically, social welfare has come under attack

9

when the economy suffered periodic market downturns and welfare reform was a euphemism for cutting the cost of support for the poor (Katz 1989). To historians of poverty and poverty relief, the contemporary debate over welfare policy extends the history of poverty discourse in a predictable fashion, with common rhetoric and familiar solutions for reducing poverty.

The welfare reform debate of the 1980s centered around the conventional assertions about support for the poor. Conservatives analyzing the recent trends in poverty and the increasing social disorganization of the inner cities argued that the growth in social welfare policies had exacerbated, not alleviated, poverty and ghetto-specific behaviors that are alien to mainstream society. They proposed cuts in federal spending for social welfare or even to abolish the welfare system all together. Liberals claimed that social programs did, in fact, lift many families out of poverty and that without the welfare system, poverty rates would have been even higher in the 1980s. However, they also favored welfare reform because they felt that the system did not offer recipients any real help in achieving self-sufficiency, but instead humiliated recipients with a maze of rules and regulations that further stripped them of security and self-esteem (Ellwood 1988).

The conservative voice that generated the greatest attention and virtually ignited the public debate over welfare was that of Charles Murray, who wrote a powerful indictment of the whole social welfare system in his 1984 book *Losing Ground*. Murray evaluated the results of the Great Society programs and concluded that despite substantial increases in spending on social programs from 1968 to 1980, the poverty rate failed to drop during this period—representing the obvious failure of these programs. He advanced the familiar thesis that federal social policies had a perverse effect on the predicament of the poor: "We tried to provide for the poor and produced more poor instead. We tried to remove the barriers to escape from poverty, and inadvertently built a trap" (Murray 1984, 9).

For Murray, the trap is most evident in the black ghettos of the inner city. He blamed the social welfare system, with its inherent contradictions in basic American values, for the creation of an indigenous urban subculture of welfare dependents. He argued that by penalizing the working poor and rewarding the nonworking poor the Great Society and other social welfare programs have been self-defeating because they encouraged welfare dependency, discouraged work, and contributed to family breakups and the rise in out-of-wedlock births. His solution was to dismantle the system that promotes such behavior and entraps generations of urban poor in their own counterculture, socially and physically isolated from the rest of society. Since social welfare programs did not relieve poverty, but rather increased it, they should be eliminated.

The response to Murray's work was phenomenal. The Reagan administration, which had advocated against government intervention all along, embraced Murray's thesis as the basis for cutting social spending. But liberals, who had receded from the poverty arena during the 1970s, were quick to attack Murray's work. Murray's analysis was highly criticized for ignoring important macroeconomic conditions that had a profound effect on low-income groups and poverty levels over the past two decades. The various criticisms of Murray's work are not detailed here, but a substantial number of reviews and critiques have refuted many of Murray's arguments and cast considerable doubt on the credibility of his conclusions.[6] Nevertheless, the controversy surrounding Murray's book rekindled intellectual thought and discussion about welfare reform and revived scholarly interest in poverty. As David Ellwood (1987, 1) points out, "although Murray may have gotten the answers wrong, he probably got the questions right." Consequently, a simmering dispute about the persistence of poverty in America erupted into an animated debate over welfare reform.

Cultural versus Structural Sources of Poverty

As the furious response to Murray's work proliferated in the media, in policy agendas, in legislative proposals, and in scholarly journals and books, two opposing theories about the sources of poverty surfaced that were highly reminiscent of earlier poverty debates of the 1960s. Conservatives, bolstered by Murray's arguments, espoused a "cultural" or "behavioral" cause of poverty; while liberals described "situational" or "structural" sources of poverty.

In the early to mid-1960s, a debate over the existence and nature of a "culture of poverty" dominated poverty literature. The cultural poverty notion originated as a politically liberal concept in the work of anthropologist Oscar Lewis, who studied poverty in Latin America. Lewis (1966) described how the poor construct a separate subculture with different values and attitudes than in mainstream society in order to survive

11

their hostile surroundings in the larger world. This deviant set of behaviors and values is then passed on from one generation of the poor to the next, thereby perpetuating a distinctive and autonomous culture of poverty. Isolated and conditioned by this ghetto socialization, the poor are unable to take advantage of changing opportunities, even when aided by material assistance.

As Lewis was writing about poverty in Latin America, a high degree of social disorganization was rocking American cities and receiving considerable public attention. Michael Harrington (1962), Herbert Gans (1962), and Kenneth Clark (1965) all described worlds of isolated and concentrated urban poverty with the accompanying symptoms of social dislocation—unemployment, poor education, family instability, illegitimacy, crime, and drug addiction. Echoing Oscar Lewis, their message was that the desperation of the ghetto needed to be understood and remedied. These authors believed that culture evolved as a behavioral adaptation and, as such, could be changed or modified. Even Lewis felt that drastic measures could break the cycle of poverty that he saw.

The dehumanizing environment of the poor and the consequences of their isolation described in these studies aroused the nation's consciousness to correct the conditions that bred such problems and to declare a War on Poverty. However, the idea that the poor adopt a different set of norms and values that are perpetuated through a culture of poverty was particularly appealing to those who were opposed to expanding welfare services. The belief that the poor were different was thus transformed into the conservative theme that ghetto residents were inevitably trapped by their own culture—preventing them from entering mainstream society through government support.

One of the first scholars to attack the welfare system by expanding on the idea of the culture of poverty was the political scientist Edward Banfield. In *The Unheavenly City,* his book on public policy and poverty, Banfield (1970) argued that the poor were doomed to destitution by their deviant behavior, lack of interest in self-improvement, and inability to defer gratification. He declared that social welfare initiatives were useless and suggested that ghetto residents had to be rehabilitated culturally before they could advance in society.

The explosively controversial report on the black family by Daniel Patrick Moynihan (1967) unwittingly added momentum to the belief in cultural poverty. Citing the increasing rates of broken marriages, female-headed homes, out-of-wedlock births, and welfare dependency among urban blacks, Moynihan described a "web of pathology" that was holding down advancement among blacks. Although his central theme linked economic opportunities to the family deterioration that he saw in the statistics, he was severely criticized for not understanding black culture and "blaming the victim." The immense hostility generated by his report discouraged liberals from poverty research that might present an unflattering depiction of the black family and allowed conservative writers to dwell on the distinctive behavior and characteristics of poor urban blacks (Wilson 1987).

Once the culture of poverty notion was captured by the conservative perspective, without much resistance from liberals, a number of scholars continued to attack the welfare system, supported by their cultural, or behavioral, view of poverty. Social conservatives argued that the poor suffered not from a lack of opportunity but from deviant values. And reinforcing these bad values and ghetto-specific behavior was the welfare system with its adverse incentives. By providing the economic means for the poor to shun work or have children outside of marriage, the welfare system was inherently supporting the countercultural norms that accepted high school dropout, crime, drugs, and unwed parenthood. Thus, welfare was viewed as playing a key role in perpetuating the ghetto-specific behavior in the culture of poverty.

Murray built his thesis on the belief that the roots of poverty are cultural. And along with Murray, other conservatives located the problems of the poor with the welfare system. George Gilder (1981, 153) criticized welfare programs for reducing the need to rely on a man for support. He described the demoralization of the poor as a consequence of a perverse welfare system that "erodes work and family and thus keeps poor people poor." Lawrence Mead (1986) accused welfare policies of being "too permissive." He argued that welfare recipients were not fulfilling their social obligation as citizens when they accept "entitlements" without contributing anything to society in return. He felt that the Great Society programs doled out benefits without expecting or obligating the poor to behave differently than they do. He proposed the imposition of work requirements on welfare recipients in exchange for their welfare checks. Mead's thesis, of course, is grounded in the theoretical orientation that it is the behavior of the poor, and not their social environment, that perpetuates their poverty.

13

The concerted attack on the welfare state had a common language. Focusing on the inner-city ghettos where poverty and welfare dependency are more concentrated (Jargowsky and Bane 1991), these writers spoke of an emerging "underclass" of dependent Americans. The term "underclass" became the new synonym for the culture of poverty in the inner city. Ken Auletta (1982) first used the term to describe the phenomena of poor families entrapped in a physical and cultural space that isolates them from mainstream culture and cultivates antisocial behavior. As Auletta explained, the underclass "rejects commonly accepted values . . . and suffers from *behavioral* as well as *income* deficiencies."[7]

Soon, however, the concept of an underclass gained acceptance across the political spectrum. In his extremely influential book *The Truly Disadvantaged,* William Julius Wilson (1987, 7) described the emergence of an underclass as a result of the profound social transformation that has occurred in the inner city over the past three decades. Wilson did not shy away from addressing the behavior of the underclass: "One cannot deny that there is a heterogeneous grouping of inner-city families and individuals whose behavior contrasts sharply with that of mainstream America." According to Wilson, the underclass consists of the most disadvantaged segments of the black urban community where unemployment, crime, out-of-wedlock births, and welfare dependency are the behavioral norms of an isolated and immobilized ghetto.

Although Wilson argues for the existence of an underclass, he departs from conservative theorizing in the sources of underclass poverty and behavior. He explains that ghetto poverty in the 1980s is distinctive from previous populations of the urban poor. By linking economic changes to powerful demographic shifts, Wilson focuses on structural factors that have concentrated poor blacks in central-city areas while upwardly mobile blacks have left these areas. The erosion of the industrial base in the United States, the loss of an urban blue-collar job base, the decline of stable well-paying jobs involving heavy labor, and the movement of industry out of the urban centers have resulted in the growth of the underclass and the increasing deterioration of the social and economic conditions of poor black ghetto families (Wacquant and Wilson 1989; Wilson 1987, 1991).

Wilson's thesis is aligned with the liberal theory that poverty is "situational"—resulting from a lack of opportunities. Two decades ago, however, liberals claimed that limited opportunities in education and jobs were due mainly to discrimination. Wilson argues that in the 1980s a lack of opportunity is due more to the isolation and spatial concentration of the urban underclass, resulting from structural changes in the larger society, economy, and polity. His structural explanation of the growth of the underclass and its ghetto-specific behavior disputes the conservative view that a self-imposed and self-sustaining welfare culture is the cause of the social disorganization of the inner city. Although Wilson makes no claim about the autonomy of ghetto culture, he does argue that situational conditions and norms restrict the possibility of social mobility. In an article on the social structure of the ghetto, Wacquant and Wilson (1989, 8–9) summarize this perspective: "Our central argument is that the interrelated set of phenomena captured by the term 'underclass' is primarily social-structural and that the inner city is experiencing a crisis . . . not because a 'welfare ethos' has mysteriously taken over its residents but . . . because the dramatic growth in joblessness and economic exclusion associated with the ongoing spatial and industrial restructuring of American capitalism has triggered a process of hyperghettoization."

In sum, the social debate over the sources of poverty in the 1980s divides along two perspectives. The liberal view contends that poverty is due to situational factors resulting from structural changes. Because the urban poor are concentrated in the ghetto neighborhoods from which middle-class blacks and blue-collar jobs have disappeared, they are isolated from the world of work and its mainstream values and behaviors. Living in social and spatial exclusion from the larger society, ghetto blacks face a closed opportunity structure. In addition, the inner city has experienced a rapid deterioration of housing, schools, businesses, recreational facilities, and other community organizations, which has further limited the resources inner-city residents have to escape their disadvantaged world (Wacquant and Wilson 1989). That leaves welfare, which is not enough. Liberals claim that our welfare system offers the poor no real help in overcoming the obstacles they face to achieve self-sufficiency and only provides minimal economic assistance to predominantly single mothers with children who are able to endure the degrading and humiliating process of public assistance (Ellwood 1988).

Conservatives do not agree that ghetto-specific behavior is due to a lack of inner-city jobs or the loss of mainstream role models, but results instead from culture and deviant values generated by a self-perpetuating

15

underclass. The conservative viewpoint maintains that the welfare poor, in fact, reject low-wage employment that is indeed available in the inner cities because the welfare culture eschews traditional work and family values (Mead 1986, 1992). Moreover, welfare families tend to raise children who lack ambition, a work ethic, and a sense of self-reliance. Thus, the poor construct a different worldview with a distinctive code of norms and behaviors that condones high school dropout, unemployment, crime, drugs, and single parenthood. The welfare system insures the autonomy of this welfare culture embodied in the conservative concept of an urban underclass by rewarding nonwork and unwed parenthood and thereby sustaining its perpetuation.

Welfare Reform Policies

Approaches to welfare reform are divided along these two perspectives of the causes of poverty and long-term dependence on welfare. Those who point to the welfare system as the cause of poverty call for its elimination, while those who focus more on structural causes advocate for the enhancement of human capital among the poor and the creation of jobs and educational opportunities. Two notable welfare reform measures evolved out of these debates during the Reagan Administration: the Omnibus Budget Reconciliation Act (OBRA) in 1981 and the Family Support Act (FSA) of 1988. OBRA represented the first major shift in welfare policy designed to cut costs and provide for only the truly needy by severely limiting eligibility for welfare grants. The policy eliminated a work incentive that allowed recipients to keep a portion of their earnings without having them deducted from their grants.[8] The Reagan administration argued that work effort was best provided by work requirements, not work incentives. Therefore, OBRA changed welfare from a system that encouraged simultaneous receipt of income from a job and from welfare to a safety net—providing cash assistance only for those unable to secure jobs (Starr 1986).

The FSA addressed growing concerns about children in poverty and the work efforts of the poor. This act imposed work requirements on welfare recipients that were demanded by conservatives, but also provided job and educational training programs advocated by liberals. The real value of welfare benefits continued to fall throughout the 1980s as they did not keep pace with inflation. Meager benefits, work requirements, and other restrictions on receipt of benefits reflected the growing conservative mood that worried about the incentive effects of welfare.[9]

Poverty conditions have continued to worsen in the 1990s. The poverty rate remains above 14 percent, and childhood poverty is reaching 25 percent. Welfare reform is again high on the political agenda, and elimination of the welfare system gaining popular support. At the heart of the welfare debate in the 1990s, however, is illegitimacy, and Charles Murray has again aroused a swirl of controversy that has policymakers rushing to eliminate welfare in order to prevent unwed parenthood. In an October 1993 *Wall Street Journal* article entitled "The Coming White Underclass," Charles Murray wrote that "illegitimacy is the single most important social problem of our time—more important than crime, drugs, poverty, illiteracy, welfare or homelessness because it drives everything else." Murray argues that without welfare, out-of-wedlock births would sharply decrease, and he called for eliminating all welfare programs, including AFDC, food stamps, and subsidized housing.

Solving the welfare problem will not occur in this decade, despite the promise of politicians, but there do seem to be changes for our public assistance programs on the horizon. Those most likely to be affected are teenage mothers, whose behavior is of utmost social concern. Short of eliminating welfare all together, current proposals call for denying benefits to unwed teenage mothers, in the hopes of deterring teens from bearing children outside of marriage or before they can care for a child as an adult. This focus, of course, is based on the belief that teenage mothers are the long-term poor and the welfare culture of tomorrow.

Teenage Mothers and Welfare

Although liberals and conservatives may disagree over the sources of poverty, one universal image of the underclass is that of a black teenage mother living on welfare. Proponents of both perspectives agree that out-of-wedlock teenage childbearing is an integral component in the perceived cycle of poverty. The cultural theory of poverty points to out-of-wedlock births among teenagers as symptomatic of the deviant set of values and norms among the poor. Disregarding sanctions against premarital sex, ignoring the institution of marriage as a prerequisite for family formation, and rejecting the traditional structure of two parents raising and providing for children, unwed teenage mothers promote reliance on public assistance and family dysfunctioning, and in turn, teach the next generation that nothing different is expected of them.

The structural theory of poverty holds that for ghetto youth the costs of having a child out of wedlock are relatively minor because the labor market opportunities and marital prospects facing adolescent blacks are so poor that, in their eyes, a child will not hurt their future chances of overcoming poverty. Thus inner-city teenagers perceive no advantage to postponing early motherhood since they lose little in terms of economic security and gain much in terms of the social status and psychological fulfillment of motherhood (Geronimus 1991, 1992; Luker 1991; Nathanson 1991)). Wilson (1987, 1991), for example, argues that marriage is no longer a viable option for black women because of the declining economic position of young black males (also see Tucker 1987). Black teenage girls may perceive that they have little to lose by having a birth outside of marriage and that motherhood may afford some degree of attention and respect.

There is evidence to support the "opportunity costs" hypothesis. Geronimus and Korenman (1992) argue for the contention that social and economic outcomes are not affected by a teenage birth, once family background is properly controlled, suggesting that it is the family background of the teenager, not her age at childbearing, that affects her future opportunities.[10] Other research shows that the costs of having an out-of-wedlock teenage birth are much less for blacks than for whites (Lundberg and Plotnick 1989; McCrate 1990). In particular, the probability of a teenage birth depends on future marital and employment opportunities (Duncan and Hoffman 1990a; Lundberg and Plotnick 1990; McCrate 1992), as women with the least to lose are the most likely to have children during their teen years. Qualitative studies consistently point to the lack of economic opportunities and life options among youth in inner-city neighborhoods as a key influence on their behavior and attitudes regarding nonmarital childbearing (Anderson 1989, 1990; Sullivan 1989).

However, most people writing about the underclass and teenage mothers have generally focused on culture and behavior. In his book *The Underclass* (1982), Auletta describes the frustrating efforts to train a small group of high school dropouts, drug addicts, and teenage mothers in an experimental supported work program in New York City. Nicholas Lemann (1986, 41), in a two-part series in the *Atlantic,* locates the origins of the underclass in the characteristics of "poverty, crime, poor education, dependency, and teenage out-of-wedlock childbearing." Leon Dash, a reporter for the *Washington Post,* spent seventeen months living in a housing project in Washington, D.C., interviewing teen mothers on welfare. His subsequent book (1989) details how early childbearing is usually intended, feeding the impoverished self-esteem of ghetto youth. Dash relates story after story where teen girls, their mothers, and their boyfriends report that adolescent pregnancy is not an accident, but an essential ingredient of urban underclass life. Black teenage girls crave a child to keep up with their peers or hold onto a boyfriend, but mainly to attain the higher social status that motherhood offers.

These journalistic accounts have convinced the public that teenage mothers respond to a different set of values and beliefs about family and work, aspire to a deviant set of life goals, and are destined to live in poverty and welfare dependency. Such impressions are compelling and disturbing. Case studies and personal observations can be very persuasive by presenting a vivid picture of circumstances that are not reflected in the more mundane statistical studies of the trends and consequences of teenage childbearing. And although these images do not represent the entire group experience, they may unfortunately play an important role in the minds of policymakers when they are faced with a growing population of isolated and concentrated poor in designing antipoverty legislation.

While poverty experts have recognized the changing composition of the poor as becoming increasingly female and increasingly young, the poverty resulting from teenage childbearing has not been closely studied. Because most people writing about teenage motherhood have focused on behavior, it is assumed that teenage mothers are distinct from other single mothers on welfare. Separated and divorced mothers are on welfare because of the unfortunate breakup of their marriage. Unmarried teenage mothers are on welfare as a cultural response—welfare is simply part of the socialization process in an underclass society. The evidence does suggest that the persistence of poverty is greater for young never-married mothers than for divorced mothers. Douglas Besharov (1989, 152) identifies those most at risk to long-term welfare dependency in his chapter in *Welfare Policy for the 1990s:* "Thus among female-headed families it is those that begin with an out-of-wedlock birth—usually teenagers—that result in the deepest poverty and form the

68 14609

bulk of long-term welfare dependency." He further validates the widely held view that teenage motherhood is synonymous with welfare dependency when he writes, "an out-of-wedlock birth to [a] young mother is a direct path to long-term poverty and welfare dependency."

Research on the Consequences of Teenage Childbearing

Studies of the consequences of teenage childbearing show that there is good reason to think teenage mothers will be long-term welfare recipients (Bane and Ellwood 1983; Block and Dubin 1981; Duncan and Hoffman 1990a, 1990b; Ellwood 1986; Haggstrom and Morrison 1979; Hofferth 1987; Moore 1978; Moore and Burt 1982; Moore et al. 1993; Trussell 1976; Wilson 1987). The evidence suggests that teenage mothers face high probabilities of welfare receipt and economic deprivation because of the various adverse consequences often associated with early childbearing (Butler 1992; Furstenberg, Brooks-Gunn, and Morgan 1987; Hofferth 1987; Hofferth and Moore 1979; Koo and Bilsborrow 1979; Presser 1980; Rudd, McKenry, and Nah 1990; Trussell and Abowd 1980). Adolescent mothers are likely to truncate their schooling, either before or after a teen birth (Card and Wise 1978; Marini 1984; Rindfuss, St. John, and Bumpass 1984; Upchurch and McCarthy 1990), experience marital instability (Billy, Landale, and McLaughlin 1986; Furstenberg, Brooks-Gunn, and Morgan 1987; McCarthy and Menken 1979; O'Connell and Rogers 1984), have high subsequent fertility (Bumpass, Rindfuss, and Janosik 1978; Hofferth and Moore 1979; Millman and Hendershot 1980; Mott 1986; Trussell and Menken 1978), and face difficulties in the job market with deficiencies in education and limited job skills (Duncan and Hoffman 1991; Hofferth and Moore 1979; Trussell and Abowd 1980). In fact, it is these factors that are associated with teenage childbearing—rapid subsequent fertility, low educational attainment, poor marriage prospects, high rates of marital disruption, and job instability—that indirectly increase the likelihood of welfare receipt (Hofferth 1987).

Recent studies have identified marital status at the time of teenage childbearing as a key factor in the length of subsequent welfare receipt. Based on data from the National Longitudinal Study (NLS) of the Labor Market Experiences of Young Women, a U.S. Congressional Budget Office study reported that being unmarried at the time of the first birth had a larger impact on subsequent welfare use than either the age or the race of the young mother (Adams 1987). Moreover, the timing of welfare entry among unmarried teenage mothers appears to have important implications for their future economic security. Research by Duncan and Hoffman (1990b) has shown an increased susceptibility to economic disadvantage when teenage births are associated with immediate welfare receipt. Among black teenage mothers in the Panel Study of Income Dynamics (PSID), those who received AFDC within two years of their first birth had lower earned income, a lower income-to-needs ratio, and were much more likely to be receiving AFDC in their midtwenties than women who were not AFDC recipients during their teen years.

A longer perspective of the effects of premarital teenage childbearing on later economic status is offered by Furstenberg, Brooks-Gunn, and Morgan (1987) in their book *Adolescent Mothers in Later Life*. In this extensive study of the life circumstances of former adolescent mothers, the researchers analyzed the determinants of welfare status among the women seventeen years after their first teenage birth. Their results revealed two critical factors: a high school education and a small family size reduced the likelihood of welfare receipt. Marital stability also protected the teenage mother from welfare dependence later in life. They further found that competence and motivational factors, such as remaining at grade level in school, having high educational aspirations, and using birth control affected later welfare status indirectly by increasing the likelihood of high school graduation and reducing the chances of rapid subsequent fertility.

The causal role of teen childbearing in bringing about the consequences discussed in the preceding review has recently been challenged (Hoffman, Foster, and Furstenberg 1993a; Hotz, McElroy, and Sanders 1995; Geronimus and Korenman 1992). Researchers now generally acknowledge that the observed statistical association between early childbearing and adverse social and economic outcomes found in prior studies could represent a causal influence of adolescent childbearing *or* it could represent differences in the types of women who bear children as teenagers. In other words, family background differences and individual characteristics that operate to "select" young women to become teen mothers may also explain the differences in their subsequent outcomes. However, separating the selection effects from the causal effects of early childbearing on subsequent socioeconomic outcomes of mothers has

21

proved to be a methodological challenge. Because social science studies of the effects of teenage childbearing must use nonexperimental methods, they are subject to selection bias or the possibility that selective differences between women who have children as teenagers and those who do not confound estimates of the differences in outcomes that are due to teenage childbearing (Hotz, McElroy, and Sanders 1995).

A number of recent studies have begun to address the selectivity issue and examine the statistical relationship between early childbearing and subsequent socioeconomic outcomes more rigorously. Although these studies use different approaches to address the bias identified in previous research, they have generally found that when endogeneity (Olsen and Farkas 1989; Ribar 1994a), omitted variables (Geronimus and Korenman 1992; Hoffman, Foster, and Furstenberg 1993a), or life course timing (Upchurch and McCarthy 1990) are taken into account, estimates of the adverse consequences of teenage childbearing are substantially reduced. While this general conclusion supports the contention that selectivity plays an important role in determining the subsequent outcomes of teenage mothers, there is continuing controversy over the extent of that role and the best method for untangling the effects of selectivity from the effects of age at first birth (see Bachrach and Carver 1992; Ribar 1994b).

In a recent innovative study using the NLSY data, Hotz and his colleagues (1995) compared the medium-range outcomes of women who had births as teenagers with women who became pregnant as teens but experienced a miscarriage, and thus delayed childbearing past age nineteen. They argue that pregnant teens who miscarry are a more appropriate comparison group to study the consequences of delaying childbearing beyond the teenage years because teens who have births and teens who miscarry experience the same selective process of becoming pregnant. Therefore, this clever design theoretically eliminates the effects of selection bias such that the observed differences in outcomes are attributable to the effect of bearing a child as a teenager as opposed to bearing a child later among all women selected into teenage pregnancy.

Their results indicate that teen childbearing does not have negative effects on economic outcomes, such as welfare dependence and labor market activity, compared to the women who miscarry as teens.[11] They do find adverse consequences with regard to education, number of children, and the length of female headship. While these substantive results still

22

rely heavily on various statistical adjustments and complicated methodology (see Hotz, Mullin, and Sanders, forthcoming), they suggest that delaying births among women who are selected into teen pregnancy will not insure better outcomes in all life course domains.

Selectivity is not a methodological issue in this research, rather it defines the very women whose lives are followed in this longitudinal study. Only women who became pregnant and had a birth as school-age teenagers participated in the Baltimore Study; therefore they represent the group of young mothers who have been identified as most prone to long-term welfare receipt and persistent poverty. Variations in outcomes within such a select group are less often studied. Yet research on the variations in welfare behavior within this high-risk group is vital to our understanding of how some teen mothers manage to avoid long-term receipt, some cycle on and off of welfare, and some remain on public assistance persistently. The purpose of this study is to examine the effects of early life decisions, changing social and economic circumstances, and life course trajectories on patterns of welfare receipt. Despite the evidence showing that teenage mothers are most vulnerable to long-term poverty, research that specifically examines teenage mothers and their welfare patterns is scarce. No study has systematically charted the processes by which teenage mothers move on and off of welfare, nor examined variations in their durations of receipt.[12] There is a growing body of research on the welfare patterns of all single mothers, however, and this will serve as a comparison to the findings of this study.

Research on Welfare Dynamics

The conservative perspective describes poverty as a static phenomenon—once individuals are born into poor families, they enter the cycle of poverty from which there is no way out for themselves or their children. In part, this belief evolved from the early studies of Lewis (1966), Gans (1962), and Clark (1965), who wrote about the fatalistic and apathetic attitudes of the poor, which became in themselves a self-fulfilling prophecy. However, evidence from longitudinal studies of the poor population has refuted the idea that poverty is a permanent state and instead has shown that the poor population is quite transient (e.g., Bane and Ellwood 1986; Duncan 1984; Furstenberg, Brooks-Gunn, and Morgan 1987).

Similar conclusions have emerged from longitudinal studies of the welfare population. Research on the intergenerational dynamics of welfare use provide little support for the notion that welfare receipt is routinely passed on from one generation to the another. In a review of this research, Duncan and Hoffman (1988, 254) conclude that "most children growing up in heavily dependent homes do not become heavily dependent when they establish their own households." In their own analysis using data from the PSID they found that although a higher incidence of dependence on welfare is evident among women with welfare backgrounds than among women with no welfare experience in childhood, the majority of daughters who grew up in highly dependent homes did not share the fate of their parents (Duncan, Hill, and Hoffman 1988).

During the 1980s a number of studies tapping rich longitudinal data sources have increased our understanding of the dynamics of welfare receipt among women (e.g., Bane and Ellwood 1983; Blank 1989; Duncan 1984; Ellwood 1986; Fitzgerald 1991; Harris 1993; O'Neill, Bassi, and Wolf 1984; O'Neill et al. 1987; Spalter-Roth and Hartmann 1994a). This body of quantitative studies now complements ethnographic research that richly describes the life conditions of the welfare poor and the ways in which the poor manage their families (e.g., Edin and Jencks 1992; Edin and Lein 1996; Furstenberg 1993; Oliker 1995). Two important findings have emerged from this growing body of research: (1) there is considerable movement on and off welfare, with most periods of receipt lasting a short time; and (2) welfare recipients want to work and often do so. Single mothers rely on public assistance when their marriages split up, when they experience a nonmarital birth, or when they undergo some other economic crisis (Bane and Ellwood 1983; Blank 1989; Duncan 1984). Single mothers spend an average of two years on welfare before moving off primarily through marriage or work (Bane and Ellwood 1983; Blank 1989; Fitzgerald 1991; Harris 1993; O'Neill, Bassi, and Wolf 1987). Although the evidence has established that the welfare population is quite transient (Hutchens 1981; Plotnick 1983) and that exits from welfare occur more commonly than we first thought, the route out of poverty is more elusive, and many former welfare recipients return to welfare for continued support (Ellwood 1986; Harris 1993; Pavetti 1993).

Bane and Ellwood (1983) produced the first comprehensive study of welfare dynamics using the PSID for the years 1968 to 1979. Using the annual data, they analyzed patterns of welfare receipt among female heads of household with children. Ellwood (1986) then updated this research to better identify long-term welfare recipients, and in a recent book they extended their original study to include PSID data from the 1980s (Bane and Ellwood 1994). Their results indicated that young unwed mothers experience longer stays on welfare and more often return for repeat assistance than later childbearers (Bane and Ellwood 1983, 1994; Ellwood 1986). Ellwood (1986) reported that never-married women on AFDC stay for an average of 9.3 years, while divorced women average 4.9 years on welfare.

Similar conclusions were reached by O'Neill and her colleagues (1987) using the NLS data for the years 1968 to 1982. They found that long-term receipt was associated with low levels of education, limited work experience, being raised in a single-parent family, being black, and having a child out of wedlock. O'Neill's work did not find teenage childbearing to be significantly related to longer periods of welfare receipt; however, she notes that the relatively short spells of teen mothers may be followed by a higher rate of return dependency. O'Neill's study, as well as Bane and Ellwood's work, showed that family composition changes were more important than labor market events in precipitating welfare entries and exits. In the PSID, nearly half of all AFDC spells begin with a divorce or separation, and close to a third end with marriage (Bane and Ellwood 1983, 1994; Ellwood 1986). In contrast, only about one-eighth of the spells begin with a drop in household earnings and only one in four spells ends with a major increase in labor income (Bane and Ellwood 1994). O'Neill, Bassi, and Wolf (1987) found with NLS data that marriages accounted for more spell exits than any other event. This result held for both black and white women, although marriage exits were far more common for whites.

Other research, however, has found a greater prevalence of work activity among welfare recipients (Edin and Jencks 1992; Gritz and MaCurdy 1991; Harris 1993; Pavetti 1993; Spalter-Roth and Hartmann 1994a). Many women combine welfare income with labor market income to provide for their families, or cycle between these two income sources (Duncan 1984; Edin and Jencks 1992; Edin and Lein 1996; Harris 1993; Spalter-Roth and Hartmann 1994a). Moreover, studies that analyze monthly data on welfare receipt report work to be the most common exit route from welfare (Gritz and MaCurdy 1991; Harris 1993;

Pavetti 1993). Part of the explanation for these different results regarding work is the use of monthly versus annual data and the way in which work is measured (see Harris 1993). The relationship between work and welfare is a central focus of this study, given the disparate research results and its obvious policy implications.

While findings generally dispel myths of widespread persistence on welfare and work may be more prevalent in the economic strategies of welfare mothers than previously thought, those most vulnerable to long-term receipt are those lacking the human capital and social networks that facilitate labor market success (Bane and Ellwood 1983; Blank 1989; Fitzgerald 1991; Harris 1993; O'Neill, Bassi, and Wolf 1987). This evidence points to single teenage mothers as a particularly high-risk group. Research consistently describes the same group of women who are especially prone to long-term receipt: young, black mothers who had a child out of wedlock, have lower levels of education, and have few labor market skills or previous earnings experience longer spells of welfare than other groups of welfare recipients (Bane and Ellwood 1983; Ellwood 1986; O'Neill, Bassi, and Wolf 1984, 1987). So although the view that people get on welfare and never get off—that welfare dependency is permanent and self-perpetuating—has not been supported by the balance of welfare research, this image still exists for teenage mothers, and policy decisions are often based on such images.

In 1989 the House Ways and Means Committee released its annual report on the federal assistance programs that it oversees, which documented the widening gap between the richest and the poorest segments of the U.S. population. One of the major causes contributing to this increasing disparity in personal income cited by the committee was the increasing proportion of children living with a never-married parent. In referring to these children, the chief economist on the committee explained their hopeless predicament: "These are the fatherless children, the welfare-dependent. . . . If you're a teenager and have a child, the chances are that you'll stay on welfare until all your children reach the age of 18."[13]

This book focuses on this high-risk group of single mothers—those whom both public and independent research on poverty and welfare single out as being most prone to long-term dependency. It also addresses two widely held assumptions about teenage childbearing and welfare dependency. The first is that teen mothers are distinctly different from the mainstream population, in general, and the poor population, in particular, as evidenced by their deviant behavior in becoming single adolescent mothers. The second assumption is that teenage mothers are doomed to welfare dependency and a life of poverty. If both these assumptions hold, then the group of black teenage mothers whose lives I follow in this study will become chronic welfare recipients—permanent members of the urban underclass. And the extent to which I find teenage mothers remaining on welfare persistently (until, for instance, all their children turn eighteen) will speak to the view that an underclass exists, in part, because of behavioral problems.

Outline of the Book

This book is structured around a set of analyses that describe and examine the major transitions into and out of welfare dependency during the first twenty years of teenage motherhood. Chapter 2 describes the data and measures used in analysis and places the context of teenage childbearing among the Baltimore mothers in a historical perspective. The second chapter also defines some of the central concepts and methods used in the analyses presented in subsequent chapters. Chapter 3 examines the welfare behavior of the teen mothers and uses national data to compare their patterns of receipt to those of all single mothers. Using these results, I develop a typology of welfare recipients based on their patterns and length of receipt over the twenty-year observation period. I then introduce and describe three case studies of teen mothers in the Baltimore Study, each depicting a type of welfare pattern in the typology, whose qualitative data is intertwined with results from the quantitative analysis in subsequent chapters.

Chapter 4 examines the process by which teen mothers enter welfare following the birth of the first child and identifies the events associated with welfare entry. Chapter 5 examines the process of leaving welfare and the routes of welfare exit. Chapter 6 addresses what happens to teen mothers when they leave welfare by examining the permanency of welfare exit routes and the factors associated with welfare return. Chapter 7 focuses on the relationship between work and welfare by examining the work activity of the teenage mothers who relied on welfare during the study. The analysis in this chapter presents a more detailed view of the process of leaving welfare through labor market experience.

The final chapter synthesizes the important findings of the book and discusses their implications for welfare policy. This chapter integrates the study's results regarding the family background, individual, and environmental factors affecting the welfare behavior of teenage mothers within the context of welfare reform debates and highlights fruitful directions for future policy with regard to teenage mothers.

Chapter 2
Data and Methods

This study describes the long-term patterns of welfare receipt among a cohort of urban black teenage mothers over the two decades following their first birth. The data come from a twenty-year longitudinal study in Baltimore that provides rich detail and an exceptionally long perspective of the life course of teenage mothers and their welfare careers. Survival techniques and event history models are used to analyze the patterns of receipt and the transitions into and out of welfare dependency among the adolescent mothers. This chapter describes the Baltimore Study, the data and measures used in analysis, and the extent to which the Baltimore mothers are similar to black teenage mothers in national data sets across time. The context of teen childbearing and welfare receipt during the Baltimore Study is placed in historical perspective.

The Baltimore Study

This research utilizes longitudinal data from a sample of some 300 women living in Baltimore who had their first child at age 18 or younger during the late 1960s. The observation period spans an average of 20 years from the birth of the child. Data were collected at 6 points, in the following time frame: time 1, during pregnancy; time 2, one year after delivery; time 3, 3 years after delivery; time 4, 5 years after delivery; time 5, 16 to 17 years after delivery; and time 6, 20 years after delivery. Information was gathered from 3 generations in the adolescent's family: her mother (time 1), the teenage mother (all 6 times), and her child (times 4, 5, and 6).

The sample is part of the original Baltimore Study conducted by Frank F. Furstenberg (1976) which initially followed adolescent parents for five years after the teenager's first child was born. The Baltimore

Study began in 1966 as an evaluation of a hospital service program for pregnant teenagers who entered Sinai Hospital for prenatal care. Sinai Hospital was located in northwestern Baltimore, an area of the city that was experiencing rapid in-migration of blacks who began moving out of the inner city during the early 1960s. The large hospital served the surrounding community, so that by the mid-1960s the outpatient clinic of Sinai was providing care to a predominantly black population. In 1964 the hospital designed a program that offered a broad range of services for the teenage parent, which was delivered by a team of medical and social service professionals. The hospital implemented the comprehensive care program through the Adolescent Family Clinic, which was sponsored by the Children's Bureau in 1964 and 1965. The 1966 evaluation of the Adolescent Family Clinic evolved into a five-year follow-up study as Furstenberg endeavored to measure the impact of early childbearing on the life chances of the teenage childbearers and their offspring (Furstenberg 1976; Furstenberg and Crawford 1978; Furstenberg 1981).

In 1984 a seventeen-year follow-up of a sample of the original Baltimore cohort of teenage childbearers was completed (Furstenberg, Brooks-Gunn, and Morgan 1987). Both the once-adolescent mother, who was now in her midthirties, and her now-adolescent child were sought for interviews. Even though contact with the participants had not been made for twelve years, 89 percent of the original Baltimore sample were located, and 80 percent were actually interviewed, a much higher household response rate than most national longitudinal studies.[1] Of the 321 women interviewed, 15 were mothers without study children, and 33 were substitute mothers of study children. Because the surrogate mothers did not experience the adolescent birth, they are excluded from analysis, resulting in 288 women for analysis.

In 1987 the once-adolescent mothers were interviewed for the sixth time, resulting in the twenty-year follow-up (see Brooks-Gunn, Guo, and Furstenberg 1993). While the focus of the time 6 interview was on the children who were entering young adulthood, the former teenage mothers were reinterviewed at time 6 and their life circumstances updated. The twenty-year follow-up interview allows a sense of closure to the life course of teen mothers who were in their late thirties in 1987 and were nearing the end of their child-rearing roles, with their oldest, at least, around age twenty.

Data on the children of the Baltimore mothers represent a unique opportunity to study the long-term effects of adolescent childbearing on children. Analysis of the Baltimore Study children is not contained in this book, however other research has assessed the adjustment of the Baltimore offspring in various social and economic domains over the course of their lives. Because the mothers' life experiences vary substantially, there is wide diversity in the outcomes of the children of the teen mothers. Children's well-being is linked to their mothers' life circumstances, and changes in those circumstances bring about changes in children's adjustment and functioning such that early disadvantage associated with adolescent childbearing may not have long-term effects on children if the mother's life situation improves (Furstenberg, Brooks-Gunn, and Morgan 1987).

However, compared to children of later childbearers (mothers older than age 19 at birth), the Baltimore youth fare poorly on a number of indicators of social, psychological, and economic well-being. Compared to urban black children born to later childbearers in several national samples, the offspring of the teenage mothers in the Baltimore Study have more problems in school and lower school achievement; they are also more likely to engage in delinquent behaviors and substance abuse, and to experience maladjustment, early sexual behavior, teenage pregnancy, and teenage childbearing (Brooks-Gunn, Guo, and Furstenberg 1993; Brooks-Gunn and Furstenberg 1986; Furstenberg, Brooks-Gunn, and Morgan 1987; Furstenberg and Harris 1993; Furstenberg, Levine, and Brooks-Gunn 1990). In a comparison of the daughters of the Baltimore teen mothers who became adolescent mothers with their own mothers, second generation teenage mothers were more likely to be unmarried, unemployed, and high school drop-outs, with ominous implications for their future experiences with welfare dependence and poverty (Furstenberg, Levin, and Brooks-Gunn 1990).

Life History Data

The Baltimore Study contains detailed and annual information on the woman's changing social and economic circumstances since the child's birth. The seventeen-year follow-up interview included an extensive life history calendar.[2] This recording technique produced a chronology of significant marital, childbearing, residential, schooling, and occupational events that had occurred since the birth of the child. Respondents were asked to fill out the matrix of information where the columns listed each year since the birth of the first child to the time of the seventeen-year follow-up, and the rows represented a series of life course events. The twenty-year follow-up interview then updated these life histories to 1987.

Gathering retrospective life course information using the calendar has been found to maximize recall among respondents. The timing of events is more easily remembered in the context of other significant life events (Freedman et al. 1988). Additionally, the calendar provides a method of checking the reliability of previous information reported by the women during earlier interviews.

From the life history calendar, I constructed yearly childbearing, marriage, residential, educational, work, and welfare histories for the entire twenty-year study period (with the calendar year as the unit of observation). These event histories provide the basis for statistical analysis in this research. During any year in the study period, the mother's welfare status, marital status, number of children, level of schooling, or job status can be determined, enabling me to study the timing of the mother's changing economic and social circumstances and its crucial and dynamic relationship to the probability of welfare receipt.

Welfare History

Welfare data are filled in on the life history calendar in response to the statement "Tell me which years, if any, you were receiving welfare including the year the study child was born." In these data "welfare" refers to public assistance from the AFDC program and does not include receipt of food stamps. All of the Baltimore mothers were eligible for AFDC at the time of their first birth, depending on the level of their other sources of income.

Because welfare patterns are based on the life history calendar information, within-year transitions are not captured in these data. The unit of observation is a calendar year so that welfare transitions are only measured between years. In addition, "continuous receipt" refers to successive *years* of welfare use. There is no way of knowing whether welfare receipt was continuous throughout the year (i.e., every month).

Two points should be made regarding the use of the calendar year as the unit of observation.[3] First, welfare spells of short duration will be underreported, causing the proportion of recipients who exit welfare rapidly to be underrepresented. Women who rely on welfare for a few months are likely either to forget their welfare use in that year or, because of the stigma associated with welfare dependency, not to report being a recipient that year. Therefore, rapid exits from welfare are probably underestimated.

Second, if all women answered the welfare question literally, welfare use in this sample would be overestimated since any receipt in a year is translated into a year of welfare use, and length of continuous welfare dependence is the sum of successive years of receipt. Therefore, the true duration and continuity of welfare dependence may be overstated, since the length of continuous welfare receipt does not necessarily translate into twelve months times the number of successive years of receipt. However, since years of receipt in which the duration was very short—a few months, perhaps—are likely to be underreported, the overestimation of welfare use is somewhat offset.

Data Quality

Furstenberg and his colleagues (1987) assessed the quality of the Baltimore data at the time 5 interview and found the data to be consistent and reliable, particularly the information provided by the former adolescent mothers. The reliability of the data was examined using the events recorded on the life history calendar to cross-check the reporting of the same events that occurred in the first phase of the study (the 5 years following the first birth). Their reliability analysis of the marriage, schooling, and welfare data is discussed in appendix A.

In general, reliability estimates of Cronbach's alpha averaged .77 for the marriage and schooling data and .70 for the welfare responses, considerably high reliability given the length of time involved in recall. In addition, many of the questions in the earlier interviews were nonparallel with the respective calendar recording of events. For example, the welfare questions in the early interviews only asked women to report their current welfare status at that time, which may have varied throughout the calendar year, whereas the calendar recorded welfare use over the entire year. Nevertheless, an analysis of consistencies in the welfare reports is also included in appendix A. Based on the life history calendar reports, the level of consistency in correctly recalling welfare receipt during the earlier interview years averages over 75 percent in agreement.

Furstenberg, Brooks-Gunn, and Morgan (1987, 161–62) also examined possible biases due to sample attrition. At time 4 (the five-year follow-up), Furstenberg (1976) found that attrition from the original sample was higher among whites than blacks and higher among young mothers who were married at time 1 (pregnancy) than those mothers who were unmarried. By the twenty-year follow-up, the racial bias remained. In fact, the higher dropout rate of whites diminished this subgroup to such a small number that no racial comparisons can be made in this research. Furstenberg suggests that whites were more likely to give up their children for adoption and that unmarried whites, in particular, suffered the stigma of a premarital birth and were less willing to cooperate in the study.

The only other factor that was related to differential attrition from the original sample at time 1 was residential mobility. Women who had lived in Baltimore for only a short time preceding the beginning of the study were underrepresented in the seventeen- and twenty-year follow-up interviews, probably because they were likely to move away from the Baltimore area and were difficult to locate for follow-up interviews. Over time, with the loss of racial heterogeneity and the more mobile members, the sample has become more selective of an inner-city population— mostly black residents who have spent the majority of their lives in Baltimore.

That the Baltimore sample consists of almost exclusively urban black mothers is consistent with the contemporary policy focus on urban poverty and welfare reform. One of the central arguments put forward in recent poverty research is that poverty in large metropolitan areas has taken on a new and unique character because of geographic concentration (Adams, Duncan, and Rodgers 1988; Wilson 1987, 1991). The Baltimore sample provides an examination of such concentration. In 1980 Baltimore ranked fourth after New York, Chicago, and Philadelphia in the number of ghetto poor among the metropolitan areas (Jargowsky and Bane 1991).

Sample Characteristics

The Baltimore Study sample began as a fairly homogeneous self-selected cohort of school-aged mothers. The participants were all under nineteen, reportedly pregnant for the first time, and coming to Sinai Hospital for obstetrical care. The majority of pregnant teenagers were black and unmarried. Although the black families of the adolescent mothers were able to move out of central Baltimore to the northwestern section of the city where the hospital was located, the majority of adolescents lived in very poor families and turned to the hospital as the closest resource and medical facility to deliver their baby.

The cross-section of the adolescents' families at the time of pregnancy reflects a typical urban population in the late 1960s. More than a third of the Baltimore sample lived in a single-parent household, and a quarter of the families had welfare experience. Most of the parents were uneducated, with only 27 percent of the household heads finishing high school. A fifth of the adolescents' parents held jobs in skilled employment. The teenagers grew up in large families. About 72 percent had four or more brothers and sisters and many of the teenagers' parents were still of childbearing age. Most of the parents had also experienced early childbearing. Two-thirds of the adolescents' mothers had been teenagers when their first child was born, 20 percent were out-of-wedlock births, and for many others early marriage followed a premarital pregnancy (Furstenberg, Brooks-Gunn, and Morgan 1987). In addition to the common experience of a teenage birth, this cohort of young mothers had similar family backgrounds and experienced the same community influences in adolescence.

The Baltimore mothers were clearly selective with regard to age, race, and socioeconomic status. The Baltimore sample was not designed to be representative of pregnant adolescents in the United States. However, at the seventeen-year follow-up, Furstenberg investigated the degree to which the Baltimore sample does represent the general population of urban black mothers who began childbearing as teenagers. Furstenberg and his colleagues (1987) contrasted the Baltimore participants to their counterparts from several national surveys. Using the 1982 National Survey of Family Growth (NSFG), the 1983 Current Population Survey, and the 1982 NLS, black women between the ages of twenty-nine and thirty-six who had at least one child, whose age at first birth was between fourteen and nineteen, and who were living in metropolitan areas were selected as a similar comparison group to the Baltimore mothers.[4] The results of a comparison of various socioeconomic variables between the Baltimore sample and the national samples are strikingly similar (see table 2.1).

The Baltimore mothers have about the same educational level as the

Table 2.1. Socioeconomic Characteristics of Former Black Teenage Mothers, Now Aged 29–36, Living in Metropolitan Areas

	Comparison of Baltimore Sample with Three National Samples			
	Baltimore* (1984)	CPS (1983)	NLS (1982)	NSFG (1982)
Age at first birth	14–19	14–19	14–19	14–19
Age (mean)	32.7	32.3	32.1	32.3
Education:				
High school graduates (%)	70.5	73.4	59.0	69.9
Years completed (mean)	12.0	12.3	11.4	12.0
Marital Status: (%)				
Currently married	30.2	35.1	37.5	32.2
First marriage	80.8	—	82.0	73.7
Remarriage	—	18.0	19.2	26.3
Previously married	45.7	41.5	45.4	43.3
Never married	24.0	23.5	17.1	24.5
Biological children (mean)	2.3	2.7	2.9	2.9
Currently employed (%)	67.8	56.1	61.5	63.7
Welfare received last year (%)	29.1	—	29.7	27.5
Family Income: (%)				
Less than $15,000	52.8	61.7	61.9	54.6
$15,000–$24,999	23.6	19.4	18.6	20.9
$25,000 or more	23.6	18.9	19.4	24.5
N (unweighted)	(258)	(242)	(252)	(289)

*Baltimore white respondents were excluded from table (N = 30).

Note: Dash indicates that data are not available.

Note: Figures from the National surveys are weighted.

Source: Furstenberg, F.F., Jr., J. Brooks-Gunn, and S.P. Morgan. 1987. *Adolescent Mothers in Later Life.* Cambridge: Cambridge University Press.

early childbearers in the national surveys, falling within their range of proportions graduating high school. Further support that the Baltimore women are similar to the larger population of urban, black teenage mothers who became parents in the late 1960s can be found in the marital characteristics. Similar proportions of never-married women are shown between the Baltimore mothers and the young mothers in the national samples. The percent who received welfare in the past year is practically the same in the Baltimore, NLS, and NSFG samples. The proportion currently employed in the Baltimore sample is also within the range of employment status for the group of women nationwide.

The Baltimore mothers appear to have fared better than their counterparts in the national surveys in their level of fertility. Their mean number of children is lower than all three national survey fertility levels. Furstenberg, Brooks-Gunn, and Morgan (1987) attribute the successful limitation of fertility by the Baltimore mothers to a number of factors. Regional differences in fertility, a smaller proportion of time married, and a surprisingly high frequency of sterilization probably due to the better opportunities for this type of fertility control among young women provided by the numerous community medical facilities brought about the smaller family sizes of the Baltimore sample.

Lastly, the Baltimore sample displays a similar or slightly higher income distribution than the samples in the national surveys. However, a noticeable commonality among these samples of black teenage mothers is that the majority remain in the lowest income category. Based on these comparisons, Furstenberg, Brooks-Gunn, and Morgan (1987) conclude that research using the seventeen-year follow-up of the Baltimore sample can be extended beyond the population studied — at least to the urban black population, who make up almost half of all teenage parents under eighteen in the United States.

The Societal Context

A further consideration regarding the findings of research using the Baltimore sample is the societal context within which these black teenagers had their first child and embarked on their life courses as young parents. The experience of a teenage birth is quite different today than it was more than two decades ago when the Baltimore Study began. One of the most apparent differences between the late 1960s and today is the legalization and accessibility of abortion. In the 1960s abortion was not only illegal but was not a realistic option for the very young and the very poor in the state of Maryland. Following a trend of states enacting laws making abortion legal on demand, the Supreme Court ruled on *Roe v. Wade*, which legalized abortion throughout the United States in 1973. Today close to two-thirds of black teenagers under eighteen who become pregnant obtain an abortion, more than triple the proportion in 1972 and probably ten times the number in 1965 (Hofferth and Hayes 1987).

The social stigma associated with an out-of-wedlock birth for a teenager was powerful during the 1960s but has diminished greatly during the 1980s. The stigma of teen pregnancy was perhaps felt less by black than by white teenagers in the 1960s; nevertheless, marriage was encouraged as a solution to an out-of-wedlock conception. The increased availability of abortion during the 1970s and 1980s has also reduced the stigma of a teenage birth by signifying that the birth is wanted or that the young woman has chosen not to have an abortion based on moral or religious grounds. Because out-of-wedlock childbearing was less common when the Baltimore Study began, there were also fewer social services and general societal support for single teenage mothers than there are today (see Chilman 1983; Gottschalk, McLanahan, and Sandefur 1994; Moore, Simms, and Betsey 1989).

Pregnant teenagers were prevented from continuing in school until Title IX of the Education Amendments of 1972 was implemented in 1975. The amendment prohibited discrimination because of pregnancy or parenting status in publicly supported educational programs. The Baltimore mothers were not protected by such provisions; however, a large portion of the Baltimore sample circumvented this legal barrier by attending a special school for pregnant teenagers in the Baltimore area.

The job market was significantly better during the 1960s for adolescents and young men and women than it is today, especially among the poorly educated. In the 1960s and early 1970s, young men and women with few skills could get a job in the local factory at relatively good wages. During the 1970s the structure of the urban economy shifted from manufacturing to service industries, and this has particularly hurt low-skilled workers (Kasarda 1985). Since 1973 a stagnating national economy has caused earnings to drop for all workers, but hardest hit were young male workers with less than a college education (Levy 1987). The industrial shift raised the educational requirements for service-sector jobs as a high school education or better was increasingly necessary to obtain a job that would maintain a family above the poverty line. The decline in earnings has made it more difficult for young men to support a wife and children, and this was especially true for black men, whose earnings lag behind those of white men (Levy 1987).

The decline in earnings and job opportunities was not as severe for women during this period (Johnson and Sum 1987). However, women's earnings lag behind those of men in roughly the same proportion today as they did in the 1960s, and as a single income source continue to be too low to support a family above the poverty line (Levy 1987). The implications of these changes are twofold. First, the economic position of black men in the late 1960s was better than it is today, making marital prospects greater for the Baltimore women than for unwed pregnant teens today (Wilson 1987, 1991). Although prospects for stable earnings and job security in manufacturing industries were greater for the Baltimore women, norms and social support for working mothers were substantially different than they are today. In the late 1960s and early 1970s, mothers of young children were expected to stay at home and nurture their children's early development (Moen 1992). As a result, infant and child care services were scarce, and other social supports in the schools, the workplace, and the economy did not exist for working parents as they do today. For instance, the operating hours of the child care programs that did exist did not cater to the working woman, and child care constraints were probably a larger impediment to work among the Baltimore mothers than among young mothers today.

Welfare policy is substantially different today than it was throughout most of the Baltimore Study period. Federal spending on social programs grew very rapidly from 1965 through the mid-1970s as a result of the War on Poverty (Burtless 1994; Danziger and Weinberg 1994). This period witnessed tremendous growth in cash and in-kind transfers to the poor. Coinciding with the initial phase of the Baltimore Study, the number of applications for AFDC increased substantially between 1967 and 1972, and welfare rolls more than doubled (Bane and Ellwood 1994). The expansion of welfare programs and participation rates was due to increased leniency by welfare administrators, expanded rights and entitlements stemming from legislation, more liberal court interpretations of beneficiary rights and entitlements, the raising of state benefit levels, and reduced stigma attached to being on welfare.

By the late 1970s, real growth in federal social welfare spending slowed as the national economy was plagued with soaring inflation and U.S. income growth fell off dramatically. Social welfare programs entered a retrenchment phase when voters and politicians were persuaded that antipoverty programs had to be trimmed because the real incomes of working taxpayers were static or shrinking (Burtless 1994). It was during this period of the 1980s that antipoverty programs were attacked by the conservative logic that social programs created more problems than they solved (Murray 1984). Reflecting this logic, in 1981 OBRA removed many working recipients from the welfare rolls by changing the eligibility requirements regarding labor market earnings.[5] For two-thirds of the time period of the Baltimore Study, then, the teenage mothers were exposed to a fairly generous welfare system: one that was expanding its services and in-kind transfers, that had liberal eligibility rules, that encouraged work with monetary incentives, and whose benefits kept pace with inflation. The eligibility restrictions of the OBRA legislation and the imposition of a 100 percent tax on the labor market earnings of welfare recipients likely affected the welfare behavior of the Baltimore mothers after 1981 as it did all other recipients.

Welfare reform debates during the later years of the retrenchment period of the 1980s continued to center on the work efforts of the poor and the inherent incentives of the welfare system to discourage work and encourage nonmarital births. While both liberals and conservatives were united in the policy objective to encourage work and self-sufficiency among welfare recipients, they differed in their explanations for nonwork, especially among the urban poor (see chap. 1). Out of these debates, a second piece of welfare reform legislation was passed in 1988 in the FSA. This act contained work requirements and job-training programs in an effort to move welfare mothers into the labor force. The Baltimore mothers, however, were not subject to the changes in welfare policy through the FSA, since the Baltimore Study completed its twenty-year follow-up in 1987.

Welfare reform in the 1990s continues to focus on eliminating long-term reliance on welfare and requiring work to encourage self-sufficiency, but the tone has become increasingly punitive and restrictive. Proposals range from time limits on life-time receipt, to wage subsidies and enhanced tax credits for low-wage work, to denial of benefits to mothers who have additional children while receiving welfare, to enforced community service work at an hourly wage that would be equivalent to the monthly payment of the welfare grant (see Bane and Ellwood 1994; Danziger, Sandefur, and Weinberg 1994).

Teen Childbearing Today

As the situation for young pregnant teenagers in the late 1960s was far different than it is today, so was the societal context of the young mother's subsequent life course throughout the 1970s and 1980s different from the one an adolescent mother may follow today. Continuation in school is now encouraged and supported by public education, social agencies, and child care services. Early marriage is less prevalent due to

40

the declining economic status of young males and changing norms regarding marriage and single parenthood (see Duncan and Hoffman 1991; Furstenberg, Levine, and Brooks-Gunn 1990; Thornton and Freedman 1983). Avoiding a subsequent birth is a priority among educators, social workers, family planning professionals, and politicians. And the welfare system is far less generous today than it was during most of the Baltimore Study years, with stricter eligibility, lower benefits in real dollars, and receipt now tied to work requirements and subsequent childbearing.

Because of higher educational requirements for jobs, increasing income and opportunity inequality, and greater accessibility and selectivity in abortion, some have argued that teen mothers are more disadvantaged today than they were twenty years ago (see Duncan and Hoffman 1991; Lawson and Rhode 1993; Luker 1991; Wilson 1987). To get a sense of the selective nature of the Baltimore teen mothers in comparison to the selective profile of more recent teen mothers, table 2.2 compares the family background and individual characteristics at the time of birth among the Baltimore teen mothers with black teen mothers in a national sample. The national data come from the NLSY, a longitudinal survey of youth who were between the ages of fourteen and twenty-one in 1979, the first year of the study (Center for Human Resource Research 1995, 11–37). To match the age and race of the Baltimore sample, I selected black adolescents who had a birth before the age of nineteen, so most of these women became teenage mothers in the early 1980s.

The comparison indicates that the Baltimore mothers were somewhat more disadvantaged in their family backgrounds than black teen mothers in the 1980s, but perhaps less disadvantaged in their social and economic circumstances at first birth. Some of the differences reflect historical trends in family structure, fertility, education, and welfare policy. For instance, the NLSY black teen mothers were more likely to come from smaller families and to have a high school-educated parent, and were less likely to live in a two-parent household in adolescence than the Baltimore mothers whose parents lived in an earlier era of lower educational attainment, higher fertility levels, and lower divorce and nonmarital childbearing rates (see Bianchi and Spain 1986; Cherlin 1992). Despite lower levels of education, the mothers of the Baltimore teenagers were more likely to work than the mothers of the NLSY teenagers, perhaps indicating lower socioeconomic status through the need for work, or less reliance on welfare income.

Table 2.2   Background Characteristics of Black Teenage Mothers:
Baltimore Study, 1967–1968 and NLSY, 1979–1983

	Percentages	
	Baltimore Study	**NLSY[1]**
Family Background:		
Mother finished high school	17.1	36.2
Either parent finished high school	26.7	55.6
Mother worked	59.0	51.5
Mother a teen mother	66.7	51.8
Single-parent household	36.6	41.5
Number of siblings 4+	71.5	58.4
Family received welfare	24.8	39.4
At Birth of First Child:		
Married	21.5	5.1
On welfare	29.2	54.6
At grade level in school	75.0	61.6
Average age	16.1	17.2
Median age	15.8	17.0
N	288	158

[1]NLSY percentages weighted, based on unweighted N of 158 black teenage mothers less than age 19 at first birth.

The mothers of the Baltimore teenagers, however, were more likely to start childbearing as adolescents than the mothers of the more-recent cohort of NLSY teen mothers. Almost two-thirds of the mothers of the Baltimore adolescents were teenagers themselves at first birth, compared to a little over half of the NLSY adolescents' mothers. Nevertheless, welfare receipt was more common among the NLSY teen mothers' families, as almost 40 percent of their families received welfare compared to about a quarter of the Baltimore mothers' families. The historical period probably accounts for part of this difference, since the Baltimore teen mothers' families would have received welfare anywhere from the late 1940s to the late 1960s, whereas the NLSY mothers' families were exposed to the expanding welfare programs of the 1960s and 1970s.

At the birth of the first child, the recent cohort of black teen mothers appear more disadvantaged than the Baltimore teen mothers. The NLSY mothers were one-fourth as likely to be married and almost twice as likely to be on welfare, despite their older average age at first birth. In addition, the recent teen mothers were not doing as well in school as the Baltimore mothers were at the time of pregnancy. Three-quarters of the Baltimore teen mothers had progressed through school on time and were at the appropriate grade level for their age, compared to 62 percent of the NLSY black teen mothers.

While it is difficult to assess whether the Baltimore teen mothers are less disadvantaged than teen mothers today, they clearly represent a selectively disadvantaged cohort of urban black youth, whose patterns of welfare receipt speak directly to the various perspectives in welfare reform debates. The Baltimore teenage mothers embody that specific subgroup of the population on which swirling conjecture about welfare behavior and roots of poverty is based. Knowledge of the welfare patterns of black teen mothers in the context of a liberal and generous welfare system and in the absence of work requirements or mandatory jobs programs should provide important insights into the appropriateness and effectiveness of current policies and proposals for reducing the welfare dependency of future teen mothers.

Concepts and Measures Used in Analysis

I employ a life course framework to guide the analysis of transitions into and out of welfare dependency (Elder 1978, 1985; Hogan 1978). A life course perspective is oriented to studying the processes by which life change occurs and thus requires a dynamic analysis. Fundamental to this conceptual framework is the notion of life course trajectories. Life trajectories refer to interlocking pathways across the life span that are marked by sequences of life events and transitions (Elder 1985). Trajectories are charted by linking states across successive years in the development of a "career" in some domain of life. Early life course decisions and different economic strategies place young mothers in life course trajectories that involve education, marriage, family building, and work. The intersection and overlap of trajectories across the life span symbolize the interdependence and dynamics of unfolding events in the mothers' lives, which continually modify their life trajectories. This study examines the ways in which welfare trajectories are related to early life course decisions and linked with movement and transitions in young mothers' marital, childbearing, schooling, work, and living arrangement trajectories.

Life table techniques and event history analysis are the primary methods used to examine the varying welfare experiences of the Baltimore teenage mothers and to analyze their movement in and out of welfare dependency in relation to the occurrence of other life course events. The information from each mother's life history calendar represents event history data, that is, data with information concerning the timing of events (Carroll 1983; Tuma and Hannan 1984). An event is defined as some qualitative change that occurs at a specific point in time and the calendar is simply a longitudinal record of when events happened. Events are therefore defined in terms of change over time, and life course trajectories are constructed from this record of events.

Event history analysis is a dynamic method for studying change and the cause of events (Allison 1982, 1984; Carroll 1983; Tuma, Hannan, and Groeneveld 1979). The event of interest is either beginning or ending a spell of welfare, and the analyses that follow investigate the determinants of these transitions. From each mother's event history I can determine when spells of welfare begin and end, and what other events, such as marriage, childbearing, attending school, or finding a job, were occurring in relation to a change in welfare status. In this way, I examine the interdependence of the mother's welfare trajectory with her other life course trajectories. See appendix B for a more detailed discussion of event history methodology and the models used in analysis.

A central concept in event history analysis is the risk set, representing the set of individuals who are at risk of event occurrence at each point in time. In the analysis of the transition out of welfare dependency, for example, only those women who are on welfare in a given year can move off. Therefore, all women beginning a spell of welfare enter the risk set, and only those who remain on welfare in each subsequent year remain at risk of welfare exit. Spells of welfare and nonwelfare are the fundamental units of observation, and their length dictates time at risk.

The term "spell", or "episode," describes the period of time between successive events. For example, a spell of welfare is defined as a period of one or more years of continuous welfare receipt, where continuous receipt refers to sequential years in which AFDC was received. A welfare spell has a beginning, the first year welfare was received, and an ending, the last year. The welfare spell is bounded by the successive events of a change in welfare status. A spell of nonwelfare refers to a period of one or more sequential years in which welfare is not received. A spell of nonreceipt begins either the first year of the study period (when the teenager gives birth to her first child and is not receiving welfare) or the year following an exit from welfare and ends when the mother enters (or reenters) welfare dependency. Women can experience spells of welfare any-time during the twenty years of the Baltimore Study period.

The duration of spells refers to the time spent in the welfare state and is measured in years. For example, the duration of welfare spells is the length of continuous years of welfare receipt. Many women have just one spell of welfare receipt lasting anywhere from one to twenty years, while others may have several spells of varying lengths throughout the twenty-year study period. First spells are all first episodes on welfare following the first teenage birth, and return spells are all subsequent spells of receipt following a previous exit from welfare.

The rich longitudinal data of the Baltimore Study provide a wealth of information on the changing circumstances and the dynamic events that occur in multiple life trajectories over the twenty years following the young mother's first birth. Measures are categorized into fixed, or time-invariant, variables and time-varying variables. Fixed measures are variables that remain constant over time in a spell of welfare or nonwelfare and generally include family background and individual characteristics of the adolescent at the time of pregnancy. Time-varying measures are variables that may change over time in spells of welfare and nonwelfare and are based largely on the mother's life course trajectories.

Time-varying measures include annual changes in welfare status, work status, living arrangements, and schooling, as well as the occurrence of marriages, cohabiting relationships, marital and relationship dissolutions, and births whose dates are recorded.[6] The year of high school graduation or the obtainment of a GED is also known. Other time-varying measures represent the cumulative effects of such factors as age, family size, female headship, and work experience. Annual unemployment rates of the Baltimore metropolitan area are also included in analyses, as well as a time period indicator for the years when the OBRA policy changes were in effect (i.e., from 1981 on). The ways in which various variables were measured is described further in table B.1

45

Chapter 3
Patterns of Welfare Receipt

nner-city teenage motherhood and welfare dependency are behaviors that are intimately linked in the public's mind. Clearly, the association between early childbearing and subsequent poverty and welfare receipt is real, but the extent to which the welfare patterns and welfare behavior of teenage mothers differs from that of all single mothers or welfare recipients in general has not been carefully examined. This chapter examines the patterns of welfare receipt among the Baltimore adolescent mothers and describes types of welfare behavior among the women who were on public assistance during the study period.

Contrary to the public impression, not all of the teen mothers in the Baltimore Study relied on welfare for economic support. Of the 288 adolescent mothers, 84, or 29.2 percent, had no welfare experience during the twenty years following their first birth. The teenage mothers who managed to avoid any time on welfare were more likely to graduate high school, marry, have fewer children, and accumulate work experience than the teen mothers who ever experienced welfare receipt (see table 3.3). More than two-thirds of the teen mothers did rely on welfare at some time during the twenty-year study period, which exceeds an average of about 50 percent of all single mothers who relied on welfare during this same period (Garfinkel and McLanahan 1986; Harris 1993, forthcoming 1996). The greater likelihood of welfare dependency among the Baltimore teenage mothers indicates the greater economic vulnerability associated with early childbearing and out-of-wedlock childbearing.

The 204 Baltimore mothers who ever used welfare had 295 spells of receipt during the twenty-year study period. The distribution of spell beginnings and endings by the number of spells is shown in table 3.1. The

Table 3.1 Distribution of Spells by Beginnings and Endings, and Number of Spell

	Spell		
Number	**Beginnings**	**Endings**	**Return Rate**
1	204	181	—
2	66	49	0.36
3	18	13	0.37
4	6	2	0.46
5	1	1	
Total	295	246	

majority of women who become welfare recipients during the study period experienced only one spell of welfare. Among the 204 women who ever entered welfare, 138 had only one spell of receipt, while 66 experienced multiple spells. Of the 66 mothers who returned to the welfare rolls after completing their first spell, 91 repeat spells were observed.

Most women who enter welfare end their receipt, as 246 spell endings are observed among the 295 beginnings. Despite the high rate of welfare exit, returns to welfare are also high, with more than a third returning for repeat spells. Of the 204 women who ever entered welfare, 181 ended that receipt, while 23 were still in their first spell of welfare at the twenty-year follow-up interview.[1] Among the 181 women who ended their first spell of welfare, 66 returned for a second spell, yielding a return rate of .36. Among those who leave welfare for a second time, over a third return again for continued support. Beyond two spells of welfare, repeat episodes of receipt are rare. However, among the small number of women who remain at risk to three or more repeat episodes of welfare, the rate of return is high.

The Length of Welfare Receipt

While most of the teen mothers who enter welfare end receipt within the twenty-year study period, the timing of endings and the length of receipt may vary, and twenty years is a long time in which to receive welfare. To examine the length of welfare receipt, I focus first on the duration of spells of welfare and the rate at which women leave welfare. I then examine the total length of time women rely on welfare throughout the twenty years following the first birth by cumulating time on welfare across all spells of receipt. The duration distribution of spells of welfare is computed using the spell as the unit of analysis and employing life table methods (Namboodiri and Suchindran 1987). From the conditional probabilities of exiting welfare at each duration of receipt in first and repeat spells of welfare, the proportion and cumulative proportion exiting during each year in a spell of welfare can be generated to display the extent and the speed at which women end receipt. These patterns are displayed in figure 3.1, which plots the cumulative probability of exiting welfare in initial and return spells based on the conditional probabilities and cumulative proportion exiting welfare contained in table B.2.

The graph indicates that spells end rather quickly, with first spells lasting a little longer than return spells. The slope of the lines reveals that the rate of leaving welfare is quite high during the first two years of receipt for both initial and return spells. As a result, almost half of all initial spells and 55 percent of return spells end within two years. As time in a spell increases, women exit welfare at substantially lower rates. While welfare receipt is common among the teenage mothers, the average spell of welfare is relatively short, lasting for two years or less. Apparently, there is a rapid exit from welfare dependency for a majority of women during the early years of a spell of welfare, and this pattern is al-

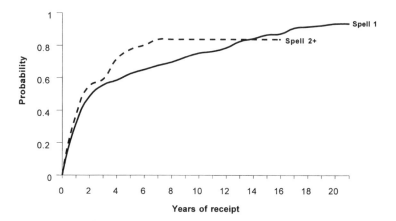

Figure 3.1 Cumulative Probability of Exiting Welfare for Initial and Return Spells.

most identical to the pattern of welfare receipt among all single mothers found in the studies of Bane and Ellwood (1983, 1994; Ellwood 1986).

The pattern of welfare exit among the Baltimore mothers is contrasted with that for all single mothers in figure 3.2. The data for all single mothers come from Bane and Ellwood's (1994) reanalysis of the PSID for the years 1968 to 1988, overlapping with the Baltimore Study by one year later.[2] The cumulative probability of exiting welfare spells that occur over the twenty-year periods is plotted in the solid line for the Baltimore teen mothers and the dashed line for the PSID single mothers. The overall patterns are quite similar. Most spells of welfare end quickly. After two years of receipt, about 50 percent of teen mothers and single mothers have ended their spells. Beyond two years in a spell of welfare, the rates of welfare exit slow down as the lines begin to flatten out.

There are some notable differences, however. A slightly larger proportion of the teen mothers exit welfare in the early years of a spell of welfare than all single mothers, seen in the more rapidly rising line for the Baltimore sample. However, among the women who remain on welfare for longer durations, the PSID single mothers continue to end receipt at slow but steady rates, while the Baltimore mothers experience more persistence. For women who have spells that last beyond two years, at every duration of receipt, the PSID single mothers are more likely to exit than the Balti-

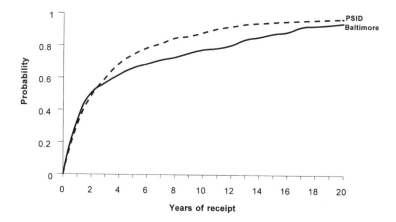

Figure 3.2 Cumulative Probability of Exiting Welfare: Baltimore (1967–1987), PSID (1968–1988).

more mothers, resulting in longer overall spell durations for the teen mothers. Patterns of welfare exit are described by a selection process whereby women with certain characteristics exit welfare more rapidly than others, leaving behind those women who have lower probabilities of welfare exit and who remain for longer durations. This selection process is more evident among the teenage mothers in Baltimore than among all single mothers in the PSID who are a more heterogenous group.

Despite the very rapid early exits from welfare observed among the Baltimore mothers, a third have multiple spells of receipt and cumulate more time on welfare throughout the study period than that indicated by the average spell length. The distribution of total years on welfare, summing across multiple spells, is displayed in table 3.2 for the entire sample of Baltimore mothers and for only those teen mothers who ever experienced welfare receipt.[3] For comparison purposes, total time on welfare among single mothers in the PSID is shown in the third column.

Viewing the percentages for the entire sample of adolescent mothers in column two, more than half (51.4 percent) of the women rely on welfare for two years or less during the twenty years following their first birth. This is a rather remarkable statistic for a sample of inner-city black

Table 3.2. Percentage Distribution of Total Years of Cumulative Welfare Receipt: Baltimore Study (1967–1987) and PSID (1968–1988)

	Baltimore Study		
Total Years of AFDC Receipt	All Women (N=288)	Women Ever on (N=288)	PSID[1]
0	29.2	—	—
1	13.2	18.6	20.9
2	9.0	12.7	15.6
3	7.6	10.8	10.0
4	2.4	3.4	8.6
5	3.5	4.9	6.2
6	5.2	7.4	5.5
7	2.4	3.4	4.3
8	2.8	3.9	3.7
9	2.1	2.9	3.2
10+	22.5	31.9	22.1
Total %	100.0	100.0	100.0
Median years of receipt		4.9	3.4

[1]Distribution projected from welfare exit and reentry rates observed in PSID 1968–88 (Bane and Ellwood 1994, table 2.3).

teen mothers who were at risk to welfare receipt during the expansion period of the AFDC program. This was a time that many argue encouraged welfare dependency and created incentives for behaviors, such as teenage childbearing, that would enable women to receive welfare benefits (Gilder 1981; Murray 1984). The fact that half of the Baltimore teen mothers never relied on welfare at all or received welfare for only one or two years indicates that those arguments do not apply to the majority of adolescent mothers in Baltimore.

Not all of the teen mothers fared so well, however, and there is reason for concern over the sizable minority who were longer-term recipients. Almost a quarter of all mothers received welfare for ten years or more, and 10 percent were persistently dependent on welfare for more than fifteen years of the twenty-year study period. When we restrict the percentage base to just those mothers who ever experienced welfare receipt shown in the third column, the proportion who were long-term recipients increases and equals the proportion of short-term recipients. While less than a third of the teen mothers who entered the welfare program received welfare for one or two years, nearly the same proportion received welfare for ten years or more, and close to half of the long-term recipients were dependent on welfare for fifteen years or more.

Compared to all single mothers shown in the fourth column, the Baltimore teen mothers experienced greater persistence on welfare overall.[4] The teen mothers are slightly less likely to receive welfare short-term, as 31 percent rely on welfare for 2 years or less, compared to nearly 37 percent among all single mothers. Differences are greater among longer-term recipients, with only 22 percent of all single mothers receiving welfare for 10 years or more, compared to 32 percent among the Baltimore mothers. As a result, the median length of cumulative time on welfare totals nearly 5 years among the teen mothers compared to 3.4 years for all single mothers. While the picture of widespread and persistent welfare dependency among black teenage mothers is not accurate based on the Baltimore Study, it is clear that teenage mothers are more vulnerable to long-term receipt than the population of single mothers.

The extent of welfare dependency among the teen mothers who do enter the AFDC program is balanced on one hand by those who rely on welfare briefly and on the other by those who either rely on welfare for extended and continuous periods of time or those who cumulate long-term

51

receipt through multiple episodes of receipt. While the average spell is short, some women experience longer cumulative receipt when those short spells are followed by welfare return. Who are the women who rely on welfare persistently, who leave after a short spell, and who return? The next section explores the profiles of women who experience different patterns of receipt by describing the characteristics of types of welfare recipients.

Types of Welfare Experiences

Putting together the information on the speed at which women leave welfare and their patterns of welfare return and cumulative receipt, three types of welfare behavior among the Baltimore adolescent mothers are evident. Women who exit welfare rapidly and do not return for subsequent receipt describe short-term recipients. Persistent welfare use characterizes the women who remain in spells of welfare for longer periods of receipt. A third type of welfare behavior involves episodic spells of receipt where women cycle on and off of welfare.

Welfare recipients in the Baltimore sample are therefore categorized into three types: "Early exits" are those recipients who experience only one spell of welfare lasting for one or two years; "persistent" recipients experience longer one-time spells lasting three years or more; and "cyclers" are recipients who experience multiple spells of welfare during the study period. The welfare system was designed for early-exit recipients, as a safety net to help individuals through a temporary economic crisis (Ellwood 1988). The system was not designed as a permanent support system, and the behavior of the small number of recipients who chronically rely on welfare has generated vocal criticism of the welfare system and controversy over the creation of a welfare culture and permanent underclass. The social welfare debates have not focused much on welfare cycling, largely because not much is known about this type of welfare behavior. While a revolving door pattern of receipt demonstrates "good behavior" in the sense that women continually end welfare, the fact that women return foretells the difficulty some have in sustaining their welfare exits. Despite exiting the AFDC program, return receipt cumulates time on welfare that may even approach the chronic use of some of the more persistent recipients.

Although all of the women in the Baltimore sample start out as teenage mothers, a wide diversity of life experiences unfolds among the mothers over time, documented by earlier research on this study (Furstenberg 1976; Furstenberg, Brooks-Gunn, and Morgan 1987). Certainly, family background, individual attributes, and subsequent life experiences are related to the different types of welfare behavior observed. An array of selected characteristics and cumulative life experiences are displayed by recipient type in table 3.3. The women in the sample who did not have any welfare experience are included to contrast with the different types of welfare recipients.

The percentages and means displayed in the table are based on column totals and represent an average level, or the composition of the various attributes within each recipient type. Thus, comparisons should be made within rows and across the columns to get a sense of the differences in the selected characteristics across the different types of welfare behavior. Reading the first row, for instance, indicates that the persistent recipients are the least likely to have educated parents, as only 17.6 percent had a parent with a high school education or more. In contrast, the early-exit recipients were the most likely to have educated parents among the four groups of women, as 38 percent had a parent with at least a high school education. The composition of parents' education among the cycling recipients is similar to that among the women with no welfare experience.

An overview of the table reveals that the women who never experienced welfare throughout the study period possess the more advantaged characteristics with greater family resources, more human capital, and fewer children, and as a result, fared better in the marriage and job market, lowering their risks of welfare dependency. In contrast, women with the most persistent use of welfare during the study have the more disadvantaged attributes, increasing their likelihood of welfare receipt and hampering their efforts to end receipt. The early-exit women have attributes that are most similar to the women who never received welfare, which helps them to leave welfare quickly and never return. The cyclers do not appear to be as disadvantaged as the persistent recipients, yet not quite as advantaged as the early-exit women, and we get some early insights into particular qualities and life trajectories that distinguish the cyclers from other types of welfare recipients.

Table 3.3. Characteristics of Types of Welfare Recipients
(percentage or average)

	No Welfare	Early Exit	Persistent	Cycler
Family Background:				
Parental education high school or more	28.6	38.0	17.6	26.3
Mother employed when adolescent was pregnant	58.3	58.0	53.9	67.2
Parents received welfare	15.7	25.5	29.9	28.3
Single-parent household during pregnancy	27.4	34.8	46.7	32.7
Individual Attributes:				
Younger than 16 yrs old at pregnancy**	10.7	21.0	39.5	22.7
Married before or during pregnancy**	30.9	21.0	9.9	24.2
At or above grade level**	82.1	84.2	64.2	71.2
High education aspirations**	64.3	54.4	33.3	39.4
Attended special school for pregnant teenagers**	47.1	51.1	31.4	22.6
Using birth control one year after first birth**	70.0	75.9	56.4	49.2
Education:				
Graduate H.S. within 5 years of study birth**	71.4	59.6	30.9	50.0
Graduate H.S. by the end of the study**	85.7	82.5	56.8	60.6
Marriage:				
Never married	19.0	14.0	30.9	16.7
Married within 2 years of study birth*	60.7	50.9	38.3	51.5
2 or more marriages	15.5	26.3	16.0	24.2
Total years of female headship	4.2	5.4	6.1	5.6
Fertility:				
Additional birth within 2 years of the study birth*	25.0	22.8	40.7	42.4
3 or more children**	16.7	33.3	50.6	51.5
Work History:				
Began working same year as study birth	30.9	28.1	18.5	33.3
Not working during 3 years following study birth**	15.5	17.5	35.8	21.2
Total years employed	16.5	15.5	11.9	12.7
4 or more jobs*	33.3	50.9	50.6	57.6
2 or more spells of unemployment**	13.1	14.0	39.5	48.5
Welfare Use:				
Total years of receipt	0.0	1.3	10.7	7.9
Enter welfare in year of first birth*	0.0	28.1	51.8	39.4
Feels it is too difficult to get on welfare**	20.2	38.6	50.6	66.7
N of cases	84	57	81	66

*differences significant at the .05 level

**differences significant at the .01 level

Teen Mothers with No Welfare Experience

Focusing first on the women who never experience welfare receipt throughout the study period, it is clear that their more advantaged family resources and individual attributes at the time of pregnancy put them on a life course trajectory that provided greater economic security than the women without these attributes. For instance, they were less likely to grow up in a welfare family and more likely to live in a stable two-parent family in adolescence than the mothers who relied on welfare. Individual attributes, however, primarily distinguish the women who never experienced welfare during the study from those who did. The teenage birth seems to be less off-time for these women, since they were older, more likely to be married, and had progressed through school on time when they became pregnant. With high educational aspirations of obtaining a postsecondary education, the women with no welfare experience achieved the highest high school graduation rates overall. Although these women married early, they experienced relative stability in their marriages and the least years of female headship in the sample. Many of the married women continued their childbearing, as one-fourth had an additional birth within two years of the study birth. However, the majority of women used birth control and limited their childbearing to two or fewer children. With more human capital and fewer child-rearing responsibilities, these women entered the workforce early and built a strong attachment to the labor market. Women with no welfare experience had relatively stable work careers with the fewest spells of unemployment, amassing nearly seventeen years of work experience during the twenty-year study period.

Background of Welfare Recipients

Contrasting the characteristics and life circumstances of the three types of welfare recipients reveals important differences in family and individual attributes in the early life course of adolescent mothers that have implications for women's subsequent welfare careers. Early-exit recipients begin their life courses as teenage mothers with certain advantages in family and individual resources. They are more likely to have a high school-educated parent and to live in a two-parent family as an adolescent, and less likely to experience welfare as a child than the other recipients. More important, at the time of their first pregnancy, they were older than the other recipients, more likely to have been at grade level in school, and had high educational aspirations. As a result, more than half of the early-exit women attended the special school for pregnant teenagers, the largest proportion in the sample.

Persistent and cycling recipients enter teenage parenthood with fewer resources than early-exit recipients; however, persistent recipients appear to be the most disadvantaged. They are least likely to have a high school-educated parent and a mother who works, and most likely to come from a welfare family and live in a single-parent home as an adolescent. Persistent recipients were also the youngest teenage mothers in the sample and the least likely to experience early marriage before the first teenage birth. They were more likely to have failed a grade or more in school than the other recipients and had the lowest educational aspirations, although nearly a third did attend the special school for pregnant teenagers.

Cyclers tend to fall somewhere in the middle between early-exit and persistent recipients with regard to the socioeconomic status of their families and individual characteristics at the time of pregnancy. Although cyclers are less likely than the early-exit recipients to have a high school-educated parent, they are more likely to have a working mother. While cyclers are almost as likely to come from a welfare family as persistent recipients, they resemble the early-exit women in their family structure, as nearly two-thirds lived in a stable two-parent family during adolescence. Similar to the early-exit women, cyclers are older at first pregnancy and more likely to have their first child inside marriage than the persistent recipients. However, cyclers fall somewhat behind in their educational pursuits. Although 71 percent of the cycling recipients were at grade level in school, which is more than persistent recipients but less than early-exit women, cycling women express educational goals closer to the persistent women, and they are underrepresented in the special school for pregnant teenagers.

Schooling, Marriage, and Childbearing

The educational distribution corresponds with the age at pregnancy and progress in school. The early-exit recipients were among the oldest teenagers at pregnancy and had the highest grade-promotion rates in the sample and therefore already had the advantage of having completed more education by the time of the study birth than the other recipients. As table 3.3 shows, nearly 60 percent of early-exit recipients graduated high school during the five years following the study birth, as compared to 50 percent among cyclers. The persistent recipients, who were the youngest at pregnancy, have the most disadvantaged education profile with the lowest grade-promotion rates and only 31 percent graduating high school within five years of the first birth.

Early-exit recipients who do not graduate high school within five years of the first birth continue to pursue their education, as another 23 percent eventually obtain a diploma or GED over the remaining fifteen years of the study period, so that 83 percent have at least a high school education by the end of the study. Perhaps because of their younger age at pregnancy, over time the persistent recipients make considerable gains in education, as another 26 percent obtain a high school degree by the end of the study. In contrast, most of the educational activity of cyclers occurs during the first five years following the study birth. They achieve the smallest gains in additional numbers of high school graduates over time (11 percent). Nevertheless, the persistent recipients remain the least educated among the recipient groups.

Marital patterns reveal strong similarities between early-exit and cycling recipients. While both cyclers and early-exit women are more likely to marry than the persistent recipients and to do so early, similar to the women with no welfare experience, they experience more marital instability than either persistent recipients or the women who avoid welfare all together. As a result, they experience similar exposure to female headship, though persistent recipients spend more time, on average, as a female head because they have much lower probabilities of ever marrying. Twice as many persistent recipients never marry than either the early-exit or the cycling women.

Fertility patterns further distinguish recipient types. The early-exit women display the strongest motivation to control their subsequent childbearing and the cycling women the least, with obvious implications for overall fertility and child-rearing responsibilities. More than three-fourths of early-exit recipients reported using birth control one year after their first birth (time 2 interview), compared to less than half of the cycling recipients and 56 percent of the persistent recipients. As a result, the early-exit women were the least likely to have a rapid subsequent birth, and they averaged smaller family sizes overall. Cyclers, on the other hand, were the most likely to have rapid subsequent childbearing and averaged the largest family sizes overall. Despite greater use of birth control by persistent recipients soon after the first birth, their subsequent fertility levels are nearly the same as the cyclers. Over 40 percent of cycling and persistent women have an additional birth within two years of their first birth, and over time, more than 50 percent of cyclers and persistent recipients have three or more children.

These early patterns of schooling, marriage, and fertility offer some insights into variations in the welfare behavior of the Baltimore adolescent mothers. Cyclers are similar to the early-exit women in that they entered marriage early, but it appears that early-exit women were more focused on their educations and the cycling women more involved in family formation in the early years of teenage parenthood. Cyclers are similar to persistent recipients in the tempo and levels of childbearing, but not in the context of childbearing, as births were more likely to occur within marriage among the cyclers. Moreover, cyclers were not as disadvantaged as persistent recipients in family resources and human capital, though not quite as advantaged as the early-exit women.

Work and Welfare

Although work histories should be directly related to patterns of welfare receipt, the relationship is more complex than it seems. Cyclers are the most likely to begin working the same year as the birth of the study child, while persistent recipients are the slowest to enter the labor force. The early-exit women accumulate the most amount of work experience among welfare recipients, the majority entering work within three years of the first birth. Persistent recipients display the least amount of work activity, likely hampered by female headship and child care constraints. Although cyclers enter work early and accumulate a fair amount of work experience, they suffer the most job instability, with the largest percentage of multiple jobs and repeated spells of unemployment.

Turning to the differences in welfare use throughout the study period, the distributions are predictable. Persistent recipients entered welfare earlier and accumulated more years of welfare use than other recipients. Cyclers also entered welfare soon after the study birth, and although they had more spells of welfare, they spent less time on welfare than the persistent recipients. A little more than a quarter of the early-exit women enter welfare at the time of their first teenage birth, compared to 52 percent of persistent recipients and 39 percent of cycling recipients, and by definition, rely on welfare briefly. Evidently early-exit women turn to welfare in times of economic crisis beyond having a teenage birth.

Questions concerning attitudes about welfare were asked in the time 4 interview, five years following the study birth. In response to a question asking if it is too easy or too difficult to get on welfare, the women who had the most administrative contact with the welfare system were the most likely to respond that it is too difficult to get on welfare. Only 20 percent of the women who never relied on welfare during the study felt that it is too difficult to get on welfare, compared with 39 percent of the early-exit recipients, 51 percent of the persistent recipients, and 67 percent of the women with multiple spells of welfare. Evidently, the red tape and bureaucratic hassles associated with program participation that is cited in the literature is felt most by the women who repeatedly entered the program in the Baltimore Study (Ellwood 1988; Rank 1994).

Three Case Histories of Welfare Recipients

Now that I have sketched out the profiles of types of welfare recipients in the Baltimore Study, I use individual information obtained from the interviews of three of the teen mothers to illustrate a case history of each type of recipient. At this point, I only present a little background on each of the teen mothers that I have chosen, as I incorporate more detailed qualitative information about their life circumstances to provide key insights into the specific topics of analysis in subsequent chapters. I have chosen pseudonyms for each type of recipient to insure the anonymity of the study participants. These qualitative data were gleaned from the original sets of interviews, including information that was not easily quantified or notes and comments made by the participants that were written down by the interviewers.

I have chosen a typical case for each type of recipient. Chandra is an early-exit recipient. She became pregnant at age seventeen, when she was unmarried and in school. She did not marry her boyfriend, the father of her baby, but instead remained at home with her mother and six brothers and sisters. Chandra's family background was typical of the Baltimore mothers. Her mother and father had been separated for two years by the time Chandra was pregnant, and one of Chandra's older sisters also had a child outside of marriage as a teenager. Chandra related that she was close to her mother; they spent a lot of time together and discussed her problems. Chandra was forced to drop out of school while she was pregnant, and she had her baby in late summer 1967. Chandra entered welfare that year and remained on welfare for two years. In the year after her first birth, Chandra enrolled in night school and began to work part-time at a cleaners. By 1969 she was off welfare and still living at home with her mother. She married for the first time in 1972, had three additional children with her husband and was still married at the twenty-year follow-up.

Alice is a case study of a persistent recipient. Alice has had a hard life. She had three illegitimate children, all by different fathers, starting at the age of fifteen. She never married, and she spent fifteen years on welfare, beginning in the year of her first birth. Alice's father had died, and she was living with her mother who was on welfare when Alice was pregnant for the first time. Neither Alice's father nor mother ever finished high school, and her mother also began childbearing as a teenager. Alice tried to return to school after the birth of her first child, but she and her mother did not get along, and her mother refused to care for her baby while Alice was in school. Alice dropped out of school and moved in with her grandmother. Within twelve months of her first birth, Alice was pregnant again and had her second child in 1968. In 1969 she entered a long-term cohabiting relationship in which her third child was born in 1970. Alice worked continuously throughout the twenty years following her first birth, though she struggled with child care, earned very low wages, and experienced considerable job instability.

A cycling recipient is exemplified by JoAnn, who experienced several spells of welfare during the twenty-year study period. Her story is one of marital instability. JoAnn was living with her brother and sister-in-law when she became pregnant at age sixteen. Her sister-in-law had also been a teenage mother at age sixteen, though she finished high school and never relied on welfare. JoAnn remained in school until she was four months pregnant, then she dropped out and never returned. She married her boyfriend, the father of her child, six months after the birth of their first child. She also entered welfare in the same year as her first birth, since she and her husband were eligible under the AFDC-Unemployed Parent (AFDC-UP) program.[5] They had a second child in 1970, but they separated in 1971 and were divorced in 1972. JoAnn remained on welfare until 1973, when she began to work. She worked for five years until she married again in 1978, after living with her second husband for some time. Her second marriage did not last, however, and she separated in 1980 and later divorced. This second marital dissolution precipitated welfare return for five more years in the early 1980s. She eventually left welfare through work once again and was involved in a cohabiting relationship at the twenty-year follow-up interview.

These three cases are unique in their own experiences but exemplify some of the common factors that explain how a particular pattern of welfare behavior evolves over the life course of a teenage mother. As the quantitative analysis evolves in the subsequent chapters, the real-life circumstances of these three women will provide useful insights into the key role that early life decisions and subsequent life events play in determining transitions into and out of welfare dependency. The next chapter begins that analysis by examining the process by which teenage mothers enter their first spell of welfare following an early birth.

Summary

The welfare patterns of the teenage mothers in the Baltimore Study are similar to the welfare patterns of all single mothers, documented in several studies (Bane and Ellwood 1994; Blank 1989; Fitzgerald 1991; Gottschalk, McLanahan, and Sandefur 1994; Harris 1993; O'Neill, Bassi, and Wolf 1987; Pavetti 1993). Most spells of receipt are short, lasting for an average of two years, but a sizable minority of spells are long term, and many women cycle back onto welfare for multiple spells over time. Once time in multiple episodes of receipt is cumulated, the typical length of time on welfare is longer, but still only a minority of recipients rely on welfare persistently.

It is not that surprising that teenage mothers resemble all single mothers in their patterns of welfare use since a majority of single mothers on welfare began childbearing as teenagers and so there is substantial overlap between the two populations (Moore and Burt 1982; Moore et al. 1987). However, there is clear evidence that despite the similarity in welfare patterns, teenage mothers are more vulnerable to long-term receipt. Compared to the more heterogeneous group of all single mothers, the Baltimore teenage mothers are more likely to enter welfare, to experience more persistence in a spell of welfare, and to cumulate more years on welfare with a longer median length of time on welfare and a larger proportion who depend on welfare long term. The differences are not large, but they do exist.

The profiles of welfare recipients in the Baltimore Study describe two extremes, early-exit and persistent recipients, with cycling recipients vacillating in the middle. Early-exit women are older adolescents at pregnancy, with important family resources and high educational aspirations that help them to graduate high school, avoid early dependency, and control their subsequent fertility. They enter the workforce with more training and fewer constraints in maintaining a steady job. At the other extreme, persistent recipients come from disadvantaged families, are the youngest at first pregnancy, perform poorly in school, and have low educational aspirations. As a result, they achieve lower levels of education, have larger family sizes, spend less time in the labor force, and experience longer periods of female headship.

Cyclers cannot be characterized as consistently disadvantaged. Although they resemble persistent recipients in certain aspects, with relatively low educational motivation, their family background is not that different from the early-exit women. However, women who experience repeat spells of welfare over the study period appear to have chosen a family-building trajectory upon becoming a mother as a teenager. Cyclers enter marriage early and seem to plan for continued family formation, demonstrated by their relatively low use of birth control and rapid subsequent fertility. As a result, cyclers focus more on their family role and responsibilities than they do on further schooling.

If women's marriages remain stable, then this early trade-off between the family and education route is less consequential. However, both early-exit and cycling women experience marital instability. Here, the early trade-off becomes more crucial. Because cyclers chose the family route over the education route, they are at a disadvantage in the job market compared to the early-exit women. With the demands of caring for more children and lower educational skills, and despite considerable work effort, cyclers experience job instability and multiple episodes of welfare receipt. These scenarios are only suggestive based on the descriptive data shown. In subsequent chapters I show the results of empirical tests of the importance of various life course decisions and cumulative experiences on patterns of welfare entry and exit.

Chapter 4
Welfare Entry

The majority of single mothers who ever receive welfare enter the program when they become female heads of household, either through separation and divorce or when an unmarried woman without a child has a birth (Bane and Ellwood 1994). The economic insecurity of single-mother families has been widely documented (e.g., McLanahan and Booth 1989), but it is especially severe during the first few years of female headship. Married women with young children may have chosen to concentrate on their family responsibilities, rather than their careers and work, and may be out of the labor force or without recent labor market experience when their marriages dissolve. Unmarried women who become mothers may be more likely to be in the labor force, unless they are young and still in school. In either case, the job prospects of female heads are often hampered by a lack of job skills, training, or work experience, and all single mothers face child care constraints and difficult trade-offs between their family and provider roles (McLanahan and Booth 1989).

Young single mothers experience higher risks of welfare receipt than older mothers because of their greater liabilities in the job market (Coe 1979; Plotnick 1983). Many cut their education short when they married or had an out-of-wedlock birth or simply rejected the education route as an early life course choice (Hofferth 1987; Upchurch and McCarthy 1990). By the nature of their age, young mothers have less work experience and face poor labor market conditions, with higher unemployment rates and lower wages than older women with more human capital (Levy and Murnane 1992; Marini 1989). Young mothers are more likely to have young children who require care. Moreover, young parents have fewer social network supports and fewer coping skills to manage role conflict and the stressful balance between their responsibilities as a parent and as a breadwinner (Moen 1985, 1992). Given that a teenage birth, the majority out of wedlock, defines the cohort of Baltimore mothers, initial welfare entry is expected to be rapid and widespread.

This chapter examines the process by which the young Baltimore mothers enter welfare dependency following their first teenage birth. The rich detail in the Baltimore data permit an in-depth examination of the circumstances of the young mothers at the time of welfare entry and of how different circumstances are related to rates of welfare entry and vary by types of welfare recipients described in the previous chapter. The timing of welfare entry is examined first, contrasting the pattern of entering welfare for the first time, following the first teenage birth, with the pattern of *reentry,* following a previous exit from welfare. The ways in which welfare spells begin are then explored to identify the crucial life events and circumstances that are associated with welfare entry. Once I have established key differences in the process by which women enter welfare the first time from the process of return entry, the remainder of the chapter focuses on the factors associated with initial entry (chap. 6 examines return entry). Characteristics that differentiate the more rapid rates of initial entry are explored and analyzed using event history analysis. Results from the event history analysis identify the relative impact and importance of various family background factors, individual characteristics, and changing life events on the probability of initial welfare entry.

The Timing of Welfare Entry

At the time of the first birth, 288 teenagers were at risk of initial welfare entry.[1] As shown in the previous chapter, 204 women began an initial spell of welfare; 84 of them entered welfare the same year as the first birth. Women who end receipt are then at risk of returning for repeat spells of welfare. There was a total of 246 spell endings, which represent the risk set for return entry, out of which 91 return spells were observed.[2] The extent and speed at which women enter welfare is shown in figure 4.1, which plots the cumulative probability of entering welfare for initial and return spells. The data in this figure are based on the conditional probabilities of welfare entry and the cumulative proportion entering initial and return spells shown in table B.3.

It is immediately apparent that the initial entry process is much more rapid than the return entry process. The steep slope of the first spell line indicates that women enter welfare at a faster rate following the first birth than they do following a previous exit from welfare, resulting in a large volume of movement onto welfare soon after the first birth. The risks of both first entry and welfare return are highest in the early years of a spell of nonwelfare, where the slopes of the lines are steepest. Over time, the lines do not rise as rapidly, indicating that the risk of beginning either an initial or a return spell of welfare diminishes the longer the young mother manages to remain off welfare.

Within a year of the first birth, 29 percent of the women are receiving welfare, and within two years almost 40 percent are on welfare. The entry rates are very rapid in the first seven years following the teenage birth such that half of the teen mothers have entered welfare before their first child turns six. Reentry following a previous spell of welfare occurs more slowly. Within two years of leaving welfare, 15 percent have returned, compared to the almost 40 percent who entered welfare within two years of the first birth. Initial welfare receipt is more common than return receipt among the teen mothers overall. By the end of the study period, 71 percent of the teen mothers have entered welfare for the first time, while a little more than half of those who ever receive welfare and end that receipt have returned for repeat spells.

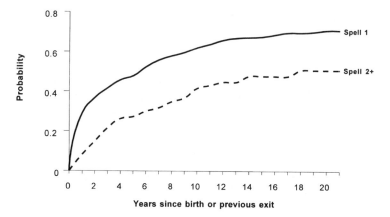

Figure 4.1   Cumulative Probability of Entering Welfare for Initial and Return Spells.

65

How do welfare spells start? What are the events that lead to spell beginnings? A nonmarital teenage birth is one of the most important causes of welfare receipt, but all of the Baltimore mothers experienced a teenage birth and most a nonmarital birth. Clearly, many of the first spells of welfare begin this way, since nearly 40 percent of the mothers enter welfare within two years of their first birth. However, most of the mothers did not enter welfare at this time, an important finding in itself. Other events that may be related to early life course decisions or alternative economic strategies other than welfare employed by the young mothers may be associated with later entries. To better understand what brings young mothers to rely on welfare, the events and life circumstances surrounding welfare entry are examined in the next section.

Spell Beginnings

Initial entry onto welfare qualitatively represents a different process than a subsequent entry following previous experience on welfare. At the time of the first birth, women are younger, without a high school diploma or work experience, and for most of the sample, without the stability of marriage. Return entry occurs at a later stage in the young mother's life course and is likely to be dependent on an array of previous life course decisions and changing life events, as well as the previous welfare experience. Our first view into some of these differences can be seen in the types of events that are associated with welfare spell beginnings.

Spell beginnings are classified by major life events that occur around the time of welfare entry. All observed spell beginnings are classified whether or not an ending to the spell occurred. For consistency, I chose a procedure to classify beginnings events that has been used in prior research (see Bane and Ellwood 1994, 53). I first looked for events that made the mother a female head of household, either due to marital disruption or to the breakup of a cohabiting relationship, which occurred at the time of welfare entry (in the same year or the year before welfare entry). Among the remaining spell beginnings, I then searched for the cessation of work. Based on the information from the work and job histories, when a mother's job ends, either because she quit work or lost her job, and she remains out of the labor force, I classify this beginning event as "job loss." Among the remaining spell beginnings, I then searched for an additional birth, then a change in living arrangements such that the mother moves out of a shared household (with her mother or with other adults) into a household in which she is the only adult, and then school attendance prior to high school graduation. The spells of women who entered welfare the same year as the study birth are classified as a "first birth" beginning type, precluding the exploration of any other events associated with their beginning year of welfare receipt.[3]

The distribution of spell beginnings for initial and return spells is shown in table 4.1. Clear differences are evident. Initial welfare spells most often begin with childbearing and marital disruption, whereas return entry is primarily associated with job loss. Nearly 50 percent of first spells begin following a birth, 41 percent at the time of the first birth, and another 8 percent upon subsequent childbearing. Another 17 percent of first spells begin when the young mother's marriage or cohabiting relationship breaks up. Job loss is not incidental in precipitating first spells, as 18 percent of mothers begin welfare receipt for the first time when they stop working. Among the other types of spell beginnings, being in school prior to high school graduation accounts for 8 percent of initial spell beginnings, and a small proportion (2 percent) begin to receive welfare when they move out of their family's or some other shared home and set up their own household.

Family events are less important among the reasons for welfare return, where nearly half of all spells begin because of job loss. On average, return spells occur later in the young mother's life course than initial spells, after she has had time to gain more education and work experience.[4] By the time mothers are subject to the risk of welfare return,

Table 4.1 Percent Distribution of Spell Beginnings, Initial, and Return Spells

Beginning Type	Initial Spell	Return Spell
Marital or cohabitation breakup	16.7	12.1
Job loss	18.1	47.3
First birth	41.2	0
Additional birth	8.3	6.6
Other:		
Move out on own	2.0	6.6
In school	8.3	7.7
Unknown	5.4	19.8
Total %	100.0	100.0
N of spells	204	91

many have developed some attachment to the labor force, though it appears that those attachments are quite vulnerable. Family events are not inconsequential at this stage, however, as 12 percent of return spells begin when the mother's marriage or cohabiting relationship dissolves and another 7 percent occur when the mother has another birth. Changes in household living arrangements are more likely to coincide with return spells than initial spells, with 7 percent of return spells beginning when the mother becomes the sole adult in a new household. Women continue to rely on welfare when they attend school in order to finish their high school degree; 8 percent of return spells begin while the mother is in school.

When there is no observed event or activity that occurs around the time of welfare entry, these spells are classified as beginning due to "unknown" reasons. A larger proportion of return spells than initial spells have unknown beginnings. These unknown reasons may involve the loss of income flows from family, friends, or absent fathers that are not observed in the data. There is evidence that these sources represent a significant contribution to the income packages of poor mothers (Edin and Lein 1996; Spalter-Roth and Hartmann 1994a). However, these income sources are often unstable and when they dry up, women may have to rely on welfare for continued economic support (Harris 1996). Alternatively, spells with unknown reasons for beginning or ending may be due to administrative churning, in which women are bumped off the rolls if there is an administrative glitch in the processing of forms or missing information and are then placed back on welfare once the problem is cleared up (Ellwood 1988). Short periods of time off welfare may simply be due to this mechanical mechanism and may not represent a true welfare exit and subsequent return. However, administrative churning occurs on a monthly basis since welfare grants are administered each month, and time off welfare usually only lasts for one or two months. Administrative churning will therefore have less of an impact on annual reports and annual spells of welfare receipt than it will on monthly reports and monthly spells of welfare. Even if women are bumped off welfare for a few months during a year in which they received welfare, it is more likely that they will report that they received welfare for that year than not report welfare receipt in that year because of the month or two when the local welfare office made a mistake or women forgot to fill out a form. Thus, some of the unexplained spell beginnings and endings may be due to administrative churning but are more likely to be associated with cash or in-kind income flows not observed in the data.

At the time of the teenage birth, family events and family circumstances are the major factors associated with welfare entry. Entering teenage parenthood or experiencing marital breakup is an emotional and economic crisis, and many women turn to welfare at this time to cope with the initial transition into female headship and to develop longer-term strategies to provide for their children. At this point, women may make crucial life course decisions. They may return to school, look for work, set up their own household, enter a cohabiting relationship, or continue to build their families with additional childbearing. These early decisions have implications for their subsequent life course and for their subsequent welfare patterns. Reasons for initial welfare entry, therefore, may offer some insight into these early life course decisions and the different contexts for receipt may be indicative of the subsequent patterns of welfare behavior that are observed in the Baltimore data.

Spell Beginnings by Recipient Type

To explore how the initial welfare experience may be related to subsequent welfare behavior throughout the study, table 4.2 examines the way in which the first spell of different recipient types begins. It displays the patterns for the three types of welfare recipients: early-exit, persistent, and cycling women. The differences are very revealing. Early-exit women are more likely to enter welfare upon losing their jobs and least likely to enter welfare at the time of the first birth than the other recipients. Although a fairly equal share of all recipients begin their first spell of welfare when their marriages or relationships dissolve, family change is·least frequently associated with the spell beginnings of early-exit women.

Given what we know from the profile of early-exit recipients (see table 3.3), life decisions regarding schooling and work seem to put these young women on an early life course trajectory that is different from the other recipients. Chandra, the illustrative case of an early-exit recipient, entered welfare the same year as the study birth to finish her high school education. She was seventeen, unmarried, and living at home with her mother who was on welfare. In the first interview, when she was pregnant, she was already focused on getting back to school. She stated that

Table 4.2 Percent Distribution of Initial Spell Beginnings by Recipient Type

Beginning Type	Early Exit	Persistent	Cycler	Total
Marital or relationship break-up	14.0	19.8	15.2	16.7
Job loss	33.3	9.9	15.2	18.1
First birth	28.1	51.9	39.4	41.2
Additional birth	5.3	7.4	12.1	8.3
Other	19.3	11.1	18.2	15.7
Total %	100.0	100.0	100.0	100.0
N of spells	57	81	66	204

what worried her the most at that time was what she planned on doing after she had her baby: "Can I make it back to school. . . . Can I find a baby sitter?" Within two years she completed her diploma and began to work. It was at this point that she left welfare. Other early-exit recipients begin to work soon after their first birth, and although they may experience initial job instability or struggle with child care arrangements, requiring them to rely on welfare, within two years these spells are over, probably through the work activity already demonstrated by these short-term recipients. The older average age of the short-term recipients probably plays a large role in their propensity toward schooling and work. Since they were closer to finishing school when they became pregnant, economic strategies involving work are more promising for these young mothers.

In contrast, persistent spells begin predominantly because of family structure changes—becoming an unwed mother in adolescence, having an additional birth, or becoming a female head through separation or divorce. More than half the spells that lead to long-term receipt begin at the time of first birth; another 27 percent occur when women's marriages or relationships break up. Apparently, persistent recipients are the least affected by employment factors at the time of first welfare entry, as marriage and family formation seem to be the early life course trajectories pursued by the women who eventually become long-term recipients. Again, these patterns reflect differences in the age of the mother at the time of pregnancy. Alice, who became a persistent recipient, was fifteen, unmarried, and had only completed the eighth grade at first pregnancy. She entered welfare at the time of first birth and stated that her main worry at that time was that her mother was sick.

The cycling women, as before, display welfare entry patterns some-where between those of the early-exit and persistent women. Their ini-tial spells are more likely to begin with job loss than the persistent re-cipients and are more likely to begin with family events than the early-exit women. The more rapid subsequent childbearing of cycling women tips the balance toward family events and results in more fre-quent spell beginnings due to additional births among cyclers than the other recipients (see table 3.3). As a result, about 67 percent of all initial spell beginnings occur because of marital and cohabitation disruption or childbearing, but still less than the almost 80 percent among persistent recipients. Cycling women appear to engage in both work and family ac-tivities early in their life course, but when work is unstable, or when mar-riages and relationships falter, reliance on welfare is a common response. The stress and conflict associated with balancing the dual responsibili-ties of provider and parent seem greater for cycling women early in their parental lives because of their more rapid subsequent childbearing and larger family sizes.

The early life course of a cycler is exemplified in the case of JoAnn. JoAnn was pregnant at the age of seventeen and was in the twelfth grade. She had her baby in 1968 and married the father, who was also seven-teen, six months later. She was forced to drop out of school when she was pregnant and chose to concentrate on her marriage and family by staying home, rather than returning to school or working. Her husband worked as a laborer, and within two years they had another child. Be-cause of their low family income, the family was eligible for welfare, which they began to receive in 1968, the same year they married. The marriage soon fell victim to the instabilities associated with low income and early marriage. JoAnn was separated in 1971 and was still receiving welfare. At this point, her early decision to continue childbearing and re-main at home added the burdens of caring for several young children, no high school diploma, and no work experience to the already difficult transition of becoming a female head. JoAnn remained on welfare for several more years until she could get back on her feet, but these early life events continue to have an impact on her chances of remaining off welfare.

These results offer some insights into the events and life circum-stances that are associated with initial welfare entry, but there are other factors that may affect the occurrence of these events, and in turn, welfare entry. Young mothers who have more-educated parents might be more inclined to work soon after the first birth than mothers with less-educated parents. Women who were married at first birth, such as JoAnn, may be more likely to have rapid subsequent childbearing and not work, concentrating more on their role as wife and mother than on their provider role. To fully understand this initial process of entering welfare, the remainder of this chapter focuses on the array of factors that affect the probability that young mothers enter welfare for the first time. I begin by exploring the effects of family background and individual characteristics at the time of pregnancy on the speed at which women enter welfare for the first time.

Rapid Entry onto Welfare

Factors associated with the woman's background and parental family would have the most impact on welfare entry soon after the first birth, when most of the adolescents were still living at home and under the guidance and influence of parents and family. Figure 4.2A displays various family background characteristics. Figure 4.2B denotes individual attributes at the time of pregnancy or first birth. The bars represent the percent of mothers in each category of a particular characteristic who entered welfare within two years of the first birth. The percentages are based on the cumulative probability distribution of initial welfare entry by duration since first birth, stratified by the various categories on the background characteristics. These distributions are contained in tables B.4 and B.5. The characteristics displayed in figure 4.2 are described in tables 3.3 and B.1. I have selected the percentage who entered welfare within two years of the first birth to illustrate differences in the speed at which young mothers enter the program by the various background factors, since the most rapid rates of welfare entry occur within those first two years following the study birth (see fig. 4.1).

The first family background characteristic shown in figure 4.2A is parental education, which does not differentiate rapid welfare entries. Within two years of the first birth, the same percentage (39 percent) of mothers who had a high school-educated parent entered welfare as those with less-educated parents. Small differences are also found by whether the adolescent's mother was also a teen mother at first birth. Family welfare receipt and family structure in adolescence more strongly differen-

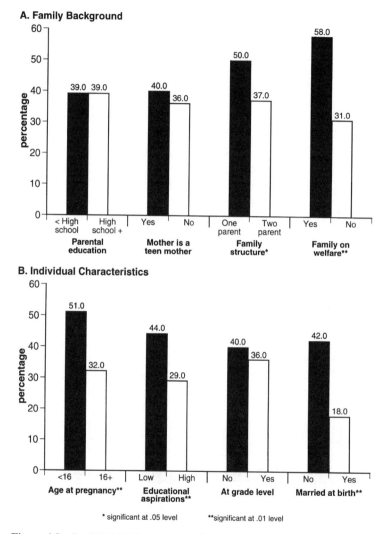

A. Family Background

B. Individual Characteristics

* significant at .05 level **significant at .01 level

Figure 4.2 Rapid Initial Entries by Background Characteristics: Percent Entering Welfare within Two Years of First Birth.

tiate the speed at which first welfare spells begin. Among the mothers whose families ever received welfare, 58 percent entered welfare within two years of the first birth, compared to 31 percent whose families did not receive welfare. Similar disadvantage is related to household structure. Nearly half the mothers who lived with only one parent in late adolescence were receiving welfare soon after the first birth, compared to 37 percent who lived with both parents. These results provide additional evidence of the intergenerational effects of welfare receipt and female headship on daughters' economic dependence found in prior research (McLanahan 1988).

Individual characteristics of the teen mothers at the time of pregnancy and birth are more important in differentiating rapid welfare entries (see fig. 4.2B). Adolescents who were younger at pregnancy, were unmarried at first birth, had low educational aspirations, or were below grade level in school experienced more rapid entry onto welfare than the teenagers who did not have these attributes. The most dramatic differences are by age and marital status at birth. Among the teenagers who were less than sixteen at first pregnancy, 51 percent entered welfare within two years of the first birth, compared to 32 percent among the older teens at first birth. Unwed teen mothers were more than twice as likely to enter welfare rapidly than the married teens at first birth.

While individual characteristics are related to the speed at which women enter welfare, they are also related to the events and life circumstances that precipitate welfare beginnings. Many of the background characteristics may affect welfare entry indirectly, by influencing early life course decisions to return to school, begin to work, or marry. In order to test for the independent effects of background characteristics and life events, I now move to a multivariate context and use event history analysis to examine the determinants of initial welfare entry.

Determinants of the Initial Transition into Dependency

What factors increase or decrease the probability of women entering welfare following the study birth? This final section discusses the results of an event history analysis that examines how background characteristics and changing life events affect the probability of entering welfare for the first time. The results are presented as the percentage increase or decrease in the probability of welfare entry as a straightforward evaluation of the magnitude of each variable's effect on the likelihood of initial welfare entry. This interpretation is derived from a measured effect expressed as an odds ratio, where the odds represent the chances that a woman with a particular characteristic on a given variable will enter welfare relative to a woman without that characteristic.[5] The odds ratios therefore represent the relative impact of the effect of various variables on the probability of welfare entry and are obtained from the logistic regression coefficients shown in table B.6.

Results from the event history analysis of initial welfare entry are shown in table 4.3. The effect of the first variable, family welfare receipt, is +55 percent, indicating that the probability that a mother will enter welfare for the first time is increased by 55 percent if the mother grew up in a family that received welfare, relative to a mother who did not experience welfare in childhood. This is the measured effect of family welfare receipt after taking into account all the other confounding background characteristics and the intervening effects that may be related to family welfare status shown in the rest of the table. So, even though family welfare receipt is likely to be related to eventual education, marriage, and childbearing, once the effects of these subsequent life events are held constant, family welfare status still exerts a positive effect on the probability of welfare entry. Holding constant the effects of other variables that are correlated with the specific independent variable of interest is the

Table 4.3   Effects of Background Characteristics and Life Events
on the Probability of Initial Welfare Entry

Variable	% Change in Probability of Welfare Entry
Family on welfare	+55*
High educational aspirations	−49**
Married at first birth	−53**
Age	−15**
In high school	+331**
Cumulative years live with mother	−14**
Additional birth	+12
Marital dissolution	+434**
Cohabitation breakup	+103
Lose job	+54*

*Significant at .05 level.

**Significant at .01 level.

Note: See table B.6 for full set of parameter estimates and standard errors.

theory behind multivariate methods, permitting analysts to assess the direction and the magnitude of the independent and direct contribution of each variable in determining welfare entry.

When the percentage change is negative, the effect of the variable reduces the probability that a woman enters welfare relative to the reference category on that variable. For example, the effect of having high educational aspirations reduces the probability of welfare entry by 49 percent compared to the women with low educational aspirations. Next to most of the percentage change values are a set of stars that indicate the significance level of the effect. A significance level of .01 indicates there is only a one-in-a-hundred chance that the effect is not a true effect (i.e., effect $= 0$) in the general population of black teen mothers in Baltimore.[6] For the purposes of conveying the most important influences on welfare entry, the model mainly contains significant effects, but a few that were not significant are included for substantive reasons.

The results indicate that a number of background characteristics are important. Growing up in a welfare family increases the chances that women enter welfare, whereas having high educational aspirations and being married at first birth reduce the likelihood of welfare entry. The age effect is interpreted as the effect of aging one year, such that with each additional year of age, the probability of welfare entry reduces by 15 percent. In other words, the longer young mothers can remain off welfare over time since the first birth, the lower their chances of ever receiving welfare.

The effect of family welfare receipt is an important finding. This suggests that there is an intergenerational effect of welfare, such that parents pass on their welfare status to their children. There is evidence that children who come from welfare families are more likely to receive welfare as adults; however, the mechanisms that cause welfare receipt to be more common among children from welfare families are not understood (see Duncan, Hill, and Hoffman 1988). Moreover, it is not clear that family welfare receipt causes greater persistence on welfare, the topic of the next chapter. Given that most of the adolescents were living with their families when they became pregnant, this effect of family welfare receipt may reflect, in part, a mechanical transference, whereby the adolescent is simply added to the welfare grant for the entire household in those families that were already on welfare when the teen became pregnant.

The extent to which family welfare status affects the length of welfare receipt is addressed in the next chapter.

A number of crucial early life course events have important effects on the probability of initial welfare entry. Returning to school to finish up a high school education is a strong predictor of welfare entry, as we saw in the case of Chandra, an early-exit recipient. If the teen mother returns to high school, her probability of welfare entry increases by more than 300 percent compared to teens who do not return for their high school diploma or those who have already graduated high school. Here we see that returning to high school is an important reason that teen mothers rely on welfare.

Not surprisingly, marital dissolution and job loss increase the likelihood of welfare entry. Marital dissolution has an especially powerful effect, increasing the probability of welfare entry by more than 400 percent, relative to those who remain married or are single. While an additional birth and a cohabitation breakup increase the likelihood of welfare entry, these effects are not significant, meaning that the magnitude of their effects are not statistically different from zero and could occur simply due to random error.

Finally, a strategy that helps young teen mothers avoid welfare receipt is living at home. With each additional year that the adolescent mother lives with her mother, her chances of welfare entry reduce by 14 percent. The parental home probably provides economic support for the young mother, but may also provide child care so the mother can work or obtain further schooling. Alice, who remained on welfare for fifteen years, explained that she could not return to school or work right away because her mother would not help take care of her baby. This created tension in their relationship. Alice moved in with her grandmother a year after her first child was born and then began her rocky work career.

Summary

Initial welfare entry is common and fairly rapid among the Baltimore mothers. More than two-thirds of the teen mothers receive welfare at some point, nearly 40 percent within two years of the first birth. Repeat spells are less common and occur more slowly following a previous exit from welfare. Over time, about 50 percent of former welfare recipients return for continued support, 15 percent within two years of ending receipt. Initial spells most often begin with childbearing and marital disruption when mothers are younger, whereas return spells are primarily associated with job loss. The context in which initial spells of welfare begin is related to the subsequent patterns of welfare behavior displayed by early-exit, persistent, and cycling recipients. Welfare spells that begin with family structure changes involving childbearing and marital or cohabitation dissolution are more likely to lead to persistent or repeated use of welfare, whereas spells that begin more often with job loss foretell brief receipt.

Several background characteristics are related to the speed at which young mothers enter the welfare program. Teenage mothers who came from a welfare family, lived in a one-parent home in adolescence, were younger than sixteen at pregnancy, were unmarried at first birth, or who had low educational aspirations entered welfare more rapidly following the first birth than the teenagers without these attributes. Most of these background characteristics remain important predictors of welfare entry even when the more urgent effects of changing life events and environmental factors are taken into account. Certain events, however, greatly increase the likelihood of welfare entry, and they define the context for receipt and the likely course of future events. Women rely on welfare when they lose their jobs or when their marriages falter, events involving economic setbacks and likely emotional trauma following marital dissolution. Women also rely on welfare to finish their high school educations. Welfare receipt that may facilitate high school completion represents a forward-looking strategy that will enhance the young mother's future economic security, as well as her marital prospects (South 1991); whereas welfare receipt following marriage and job loss is a response strategy, born out of economic necessity and leaving an early mark of instability in a young mother's life.

The process by which the Baltimore mothers entered welfare following the first birth is conditioned by the age and marital status of the young mother at first birth. An older age at pregnancy places the mother closer to high school completion, with more human capital and in a better position to eventually find work and be self-supporting. Being married at first birth seems to protect the young mother from welfare receipt, but the stability of early marriages are fragile (see Furstenberg, Brooks-Gunn, and Morgan 1987; Furstenberg 1988). When young marriages dissolve, women who chose to concentrate more on their domestic and family roles than on developing their human capital and work roles during marriage may face greater obstacles to self-reliance as female heads than women who followed an early education or work trajectory. This appears to be an emerging pattern among the cycling recipients, for instance, who married early, had rapid subsequent childbearing, and who experienced considerable marital instability. They then entered female headship with more children, less education, and less work experience than other teenage mothers who lived at home, went back to school, or delayed subsequent childbearing. The relevance of these early life course decisions for the length of welfare receipt and the permanence of welfare exits should emerge in subsequent analyses.

Chapter 5
Routes of Welfare Exit

Social concern over teenage childbearing and welfare centers on the extent to which welfare receipt is persistent. In chapter 4, it was shown that initial welfare entry was both common and fairly rapid, a finding that was not unexpected given the composition of the Baltimore mothers and given the defining event of this cohort, an early premarital birth. The welfare system was designed to help out families in times of crisis, and transitions into female headship as a teenager or following marital dissolution are such times (Bane and Ellwood 1994). It makes sense that welfare receipt is more common among young mothers and among those with the greatest obstacles to becoming self-sufficient, at least in the short run. Furthermore, there is public understanding and considerable tolerance for the need to rely on welfare during times of crisis, but tolerance wanes and public outcry elevates when receipt becomes long term and reliance on welfare seems to be a way of life (Heclo 1994).

The extent to which this occurs among the Baltimore mothers is addressed in chapter 3. The patterns of welfare receipt among the Baltimore mothers are similar to the patterns found among all single mothers. Most spells of welfare are short, averaging two years, though about a third of the mothers who end receipt return for repeat spells of welfare. Return spells end even more rapidly than initial spells. Once the cumulative time on welfare is tallied, the Baltimore mothers average nearly five years of welfare receipt over the twenty-year study period, exhibiting somewhat greater reliance on welfare than single mothers as a whole, which is consistent with most of the literature on teenage mothers and welfare receipt. Although most welfare experiences are brief, other experiences substantiate the cause for social and fiscal concern. A sizable minority of the mothers remain on welfare long term, and another group of mothers have repeated episodes of receipt, cycling on and off of welfare over time. This chapter presents a detailed analysis of these patterns of welfare receipt by examining the process by which mothers leave welfare dependency and identifying the factors and events associated with the length of welfare spells.

A number of previous studies analyzing longitudinal data report consistent findings regarding the determinants of welfare exits. Although the data sources are diverse, ranging from national samples (e.g., Bane and Ellwood, 1983; 1994; Blank 1989; Coe 1979; Ellwood 1986; Fitzgerald 1991; Hutchens 1981; O'Neill, Bassi, and Wolf 1987) to caseload data (e.g., O'Neill et al. 1984; Rank 1986; 1994; Wiseman 1977) to specific program and demonstration populations (e.g., Maynard 1993; Plotnick 1983), most studies have concentrated on female-headed families and have examined the effects of individual characteristics and the contextual effects of program parameters and labor market conditions on the probability of moving off welfare.[1]

In general, the studies find significant age, race, education, work experience, and family size effects, and for those that study the impact of family structure, significant effects of female headship. Program parameters, such as eligibility restrictions and the value of AFDC benefits, and local labor market conditions, such as unemployment rates, are also found to influence the speed at which women exit the welfare system. In particular, black female heads, women with no previous work experience, and women with many children have lower probabilities of exiting welfare and longer periods of welfare receipt. Once again, previous research has identified the sample of black teenage mothers in the Baltimore study as the group of welfare recipients most prone to long-term and repeated receipt. Moreover, it is largely on this group of young inner-city minority mothers that welfare policy and welfare debates focus.

The welfare research has concentrated primarily on identifying longterm recipients, their characteristics, and the life circumstances that lead to persistent dependency (e.g., Besharov 1989; Ellwood 1986). Less research attention has focused on variations within the group targeted for long-term receipt, such as teenage mothers. Yet, knowledge about the welfare dynamics of inner-city teenage mothers is indispensable to understanding the processes that lead to persistent welfare dependence and how some young mothers avoid long-term receipt in spite of their age and limited human capital and their often disadvantaged environments. I begin to explore variations in welfare dynamics by examining background characteristics that differentiate the length of welfare spells.

Rapid Exits from Welfare

We learned in chapter 3 that 50 percent of all first spells and 55 percent of all return spells of welfare end within two years. To examine whether certain characteristics differentiate those mothers who exit welfare rapidly from those who experience more persistence on the program, I use the percentage of mothers who have exited welfare within two years of beginning a spell to define rapid exits. Again, I examine the family background characteristics and individual attributes at the time of pregnancy or first birth (see fig. 5.1). For these comparisons, all spells are pooled.

Mothers who have a high school-educated parent, whose mothers were not teen parents, who lived in a two-parent family in adolescence, or whose family did not receive welfare were more likely to exit welfare rapidly within the first two years of receipt than the mothers without these attributes (see fig. 5.1A). The largest differences appear by parental education and intergenerational teen childbearing. Among mothers with a high school-educated parent, 58 percent ended their welfare spells within two years, compared to 47 percent among the mothers with less-educated parents. Teen mothers whose own mother was also a teen parent are slower to exit welfare, as 45 percent end receipt within two years, compared to 58 percent among the adolescent mothers whose mothers were not teen parents.

Although family welfare receipt differentiated the speed at which mothers entered welfare (see chap. 4), it has far less impact on the rate of welfare exit. The small differences shown in figure 5.1A are not statistically significant, meaning that mothers who experienced welfare in childhood are no less likely to exit welfare rapidly than the mothers whose families did not receive welfare. While family background may impinge more immediately on the process of initial welfare entry, its effects become more remote once women enter welfare and develop strategies for leaving. The effects of family background and individual characteristics probably influence decisions involved in developing different economic strategies, which may in turn facilitate or hamper rapid wel-

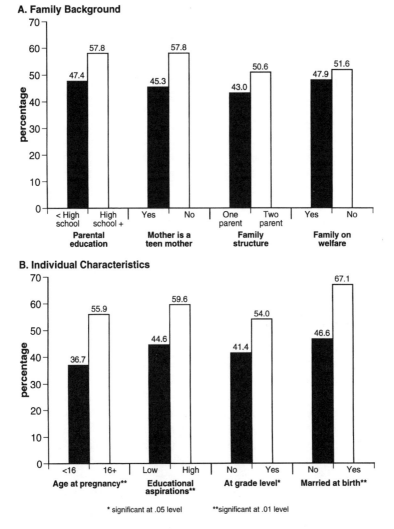

Figure 5.1 Rapid Exits by Background Characteristics: Percent Exiting Welfare within Two Years of Receipt.

fare exit. Thus, background characteristics are likely to impact the rate of welfare exit indirectly, by affecting key life course decisions and intervening events that occur after women enter welfare and engage in the process of leaving welfare.

The effects of individual characteristics at the time of pregnancy or first birth on the speed of welfare exit are shown in figure 5.1B. The age at which the adolescent became pregnant has an impact on how rapidly the young parent is able to end welfare receipt. Among the teenagers who were less than sixteen at pregnancy, 37 percent leave welfare within two years of beginning a spell, while 56 percent of the older teen mothers end receipt within two years. Unwed mothers at first birth experience longer stays on welfare than married mothers. Only 47 percent of the teen mothers who were unmarried at first birth exit welfare within two years of receipt, compared to 67 percent among the married mothers. Mothers who expressed high educational aspirations when they were pregnant teenagers also experienced a more rapid exit from welfare than mothers who were less motivated educationally. Finally, the teenage mothers who were at the appropriate grade level in school when they became pregnant exited welfare more rapidly than the teenagers who had repeated grades in school.

Routes of Welfare Exit

The timing and speed of welfare exits by characteristics of the mothers tell us about variations in the length of welfare spells and are one important aspect of the welfare dynamics of the Baltimore mothers. Another key aspect is how women end receipt. The ways in which welfare spells end give us insights into the different strategies young mothers employ to get back on their feet and support their families off welfare. We can also observe which routes of exit are more permanent and which lead to welfare return by examining the spell endings of the different recipient types, defined by their patterns of receipt over the study.

The distribution of spell endings by type of welfare recipient for all endings observed in the data is displayed in table 5.1. The procedure used to define ending events is similar to and consistent with the procedure used to define beginning events. Around the time of welfare exit, I first searched for marriage or relationship changes, then for employment changes, and then for changes in household living arrangements among those who do not experience a family structure change. Marriage and relationship events are prioritized over women's work events because of the greater potential economic security associated with men's employment and with earnings through a spouse or partner than that associated with women's earnings, at least during most of this time period (Levy and Murnane 1992; Marini 1989).[2] One event that precludes searching for any others is when the youngest child turns eighteen and the mother is no longer eligible for welfare. All spells are pooled, but note that only cyclers experience return spells of welfare.

Focusing on the distribution of all spell endings shown in the first column of table 5.1, we see that the two most common ways women leave welfare are through work or through marriage or cohabitation. Work is overwhelmingly more important than any other event in facilitating welfare exits. More than 60 percent of all observed spell endings occurred when the young mother either found a job, thus ceased being unemployed, or changed jobs. A change in jobs could mean higher wages, more hours of work, or both, increasing mothers' income and moving them off welfare.

This greater prevalence of work associated with welfare exits is not unique to the Baltimore data. Other studies that have examined monthly reports of work status around the time of welfare exit also find that the majority of exits occur through work (e.g., Gritz and MaCurdy 1991; Harris 1993; Pavetti 1993; Spalter-Roth and Hartmann 1994a). How-

Table 5.1   Percent Distribution of Spell Endings by Recipient Type

		Recipient Type		
Ending Type	**All Spells**	**Early Exit**	**Persistent**	**Cycler**
Marriage or cohabitation	20.7	12.5	22.0	23.7
Work	62.6	64.3	67.8	59.5
Other:				
Youngest child turns 18	2.9	3.6	1.7	3.1
Move back in with family	4.1	1.8	5.1	4.6
Unknown	9.8	17.9	3.4	9.2
Total %	100.0	100.0	100.0	100.0
N of spells	246	56	59	131

ever, Bane and Ellwood's influential work on welfare dynamics consistently reports a lower percentage of spell endings due to earnings increases.[3] Their 1994 reanalysis of the PSID finds that 25 percent of welfare exits are associated with increases in the earnings of the single mother, which is a higher percentage than that reported in their earlier work (Bane and Ellwood 1983; Ellwood 1986), but still lower than that found in the Baltimore data. Some of this difference is due to the way in which work exits are defined (see chap. 7, which examines the work activity of welfare mothers).

The second most common route out of dependency is through marriage or sharing a household with a steady boyfriend. Over 20 percent of observed exits occurred when the young mother married or moved in with a partner, three-fifths involving marriage and two-fifths cohabitation. Marriage is a less common exit route than work, reflecting the lower marriage or cohabitation rates of black women and the secular decline in marriage rates overall beginning in the 1970s (Bane and Ellwood 1983; Lichter et al. 1992; Mare and Winship 1991). The remaining exits occurred less frequently. A small percentage of spell endings (2.9 percent) occurred when mothers were no longer eligible for welfare because their children were all older than eighteen. This event is fairly rare and could have occurred only to those mothers who had one child or who had two children spaced close together, since the oldest child must be at least twenty by the end of the study period. Some spells end when the mother moves back in with her family (4.1 percent), and about 10 percent of endings are not linked with any obvious life event or status. As mentioned in chapter 4, these unknown exits may be associated with income sources not recorded in the data, such as money from family, friends, or the absent father and possibly his family.

The distribution of endings by recipient type shown in the remaining columns of table 5.1 reveals that early-exit women are more likely to end their spells through a job and less likely to exit through marriage. In contrast, cyclers are more likely to exit welfare through marriage or a live-in relationship and less likely to end welfare through work than the other recipients. Although persistent recipients rely on welfare for longer periods of time than the other recipients, they eventually end receipt primarily through work and, to a lesser degree, though more than early-exit women, through marriage. Almost 20 percent of the spell endings of early-exit women are unexplained, suggesting that their endings are disproportionately associated with additional income sources or with administrative mechanisms. The fact that early-exit women do not return to welfare again once they leave, however, makes the administrative explanation less probable.

Knowing that, by definition, early-exit and persistent recipients experience only one spell of welfare and do not return, the greater prevalence of work exits among these types of recipients suggests that the work route is a more permanent exit from welfare than the marriage route, which is more common among cyclers. Although persistent women end receipt through marriage to nearly the same degree as cyclers, keep in mind that their exits occur after a longer period of welfare receipt (the spells of persistent recipients are longer on average than the spells of cyclers) and marriage, overall, is less frequent among the persistent recipients (see table 3.3). Therefore, not only does the marriage route seem to result in more returns to welfare but also appears to be a slower process of leaving welfare.

The three case histories of recipients reflect these overall patterns. Although Chandra entered welfare in 1967, at the time of the study birth, she relied on welfare so that she could return to high school. She returned to night school one month after her first birth and worked part-time at a cleaners pressing clothes. By 1969 she completed her high school degree and left welfare by obtaining a full-time job as a typist. This strategy seemed to be especially successful since, although she was unmarried until 1972, she continued to work throughout the rest of the study period and never returned to welfare.

Alice, a persistent recipient who relied on welfare for fifteen years beginning with the birth of the study child, left welfare through work as well. Although Alice never married, she was in a long-term relationship with a man she lived with for fourteen years, during most of the time that she was on welfare. Evidently, this relationship did not provide Alice the economic security needed to leave welfare or to marry (Wilson 1987). Alice returned to school twice, once for four months and a second time for three months, but she never obtained more than a tenth-grade education. She explained that the lack of child care and the demands of young children prevented her from continuing in school. Alice worked throughout most of the time she was on welfare, stopping for a few years when she felt overwhelmed with the responsibilities of caring for three young children. But not until 1980 she was able to leave welfare through work.

Alice is a classic portrait of a persistent recipient who never married, never finished high school, and had three children by the age of nineteen. Despite these obvious constraints for finding work that pays a decent wage, nonwork does not describe this recipient, nor is it characteristic of persistent recipients overall.

JoAnn, who displayed cycling welfare behavior in the study, ended her first welfare spell of six years by entering a cohabiting relationship in 1974. This enabled her to leave welfare, and she soon began to work as well. She married her partner in 1978, but the relationship began to falter the next year and they separated in 1980. Struggling with her marriage and the prospects of becoming a female head again, she quit work in 1979 and returned to welfare for a second spell. Now a female head, but with older children, she returned to work in 1985 and left welfare. Although work was the eventual way that JoAnn was able to end receipt, she began her work career later than most of the teen mothers, in 1974 after her first marriage fell apart. Economic strategies involving marriage or cohabitation in the absence of work or further schooling can leave the young mother economically vulnerable if the relationship does not remain stable. The marital instability in JoAnn's early years as a parent led to her repeated use of welfare, with the first exit through cohabitation less permanent than the subsequent work exit.

The Relationship between Beginnings and Endings

We now ask whether the way in which welfare spells end is associated with the way in which spells begin. Table 5.2 examines the relationship between spell beginnings and spell endings for all spells. The less-frequent endings and beginnings involving household changes in living arrangements, school attendance, and the aging of children have been collapsed into an "other" category along with the unexplained endings and beginnings. The information in the table shows the extent to which a particular spell beginning results in a distribution of spell endings that is different from other beginning types and different from the overall total distribution of endings shown in table 5.1.

For instance, among all spells that begin with marital or cohabitation dissolution, 26 percent end with a new marriage or a new live-in relationship; 51 percent end with work; and 23 percent end in other ways. Clearly, work endings are more prevalent, but compared to the other spell beginnings, spells that begin when relationships break up end with the formation of new marital or cohabiting relationships, more so than the overall total of 21 percent, and more so than other spell beginnings.

This same pattern is observed for spell beginnings involving job loss. Welfare spells that begin when the mother stops working are more likely to end with a new job and less likely to end through marriage or cohabitation or through other ways compared to the other types of spell beginnings. It is apparent that the ways in which welfare spells begin and end disproportionately occur within the same life context, implying a sense of inertia along early life course trajectories. We see further that spells that begin with childbearing are more likely to end with marriage or cohabitation, continuing along a family route.

Note also that spells that end in other ways are overrepresented among beginnings that occur for other reasons, again suggesting that income flows from relatives, boyfriends, or friends that fluctuate over time may explain movement on and off of welfare when no other obvious life event occurs. Nevertheless, work is the dominant route of exit for spells that begin in other ways, probably ending welfare receipt that occurs because of school attendance or residential moves.

The pattern of association between beginning and ending types is evident in table 5.2, but the relationships are relatively mild. On the other hand, the predominance of work in facilitating welfare exits of all beginnings is overwhelmingly apparent. In general, welfare spells that begin with family structure changes involving marital or cohabitation breakup and additional childbearing are least likely to end through work, indicating that the work route is especially difficult for women with young children. But even among welfare spells that begin in the same

Table 5.2   Percent Distribution of Spell Endings by Type of Spell Beginning

Ending Type	Beginning Type				
	Marital/ Cohab Breakup	Job Loss	First Birth	Additional Birth	Other
Marriage or cohabitation	25.7	20.0	23.0	22.7	14.0
Work	51.4	69.2	66.2	54.6	60.0
Other	22.9	10.8	10.8	22.7	26.0
Total %	100.0	100.0	100.0	100.0	100.0
N of spells	35	65	74	22	50

year as the study birth, nearly two-thirds of all recipients left welfare through work. The three case histories of welfare recipients fit this overall pattern. Though all three entered welfare in the same year at first birth, two out of three, Chandra and Alice, left welfare through work, while the third, JoAnn, exited her initial spell of welfare through a relationship.

The distributions in table 5.2 do not include information about the timing of spells or the length of receipt, but do suggest a sense of continuity in certain early life course trajectories. Putting together what we have learned about the rate at which welfare spells end and the characteristics and events that are associated with welfare exits, we now move to the multivariate context to explain how the probability of leaving welfare depends on background factors and the changing family, social, and economic environment of the young mother over time.

The Determinants of the Transition Off Welfare

The process by which the Baltimore mothers exit the welfare program is analyzed using event history methods, in a similar manner to that shown in chapter 4 on welfare entry. Using a life course framework, a model containing background characteristics and key events and changing circumstances that occur to the mother over her parental life course, is estimated to predict welfare exits. The parameter estimates from the logistic regression are shown in table B.9. The effects of various variables in the model on the probability of welfare exit are again displayed as the percentage change in the odds of leaving welfare for mothers with a particular characteristic, or who experience a particular event relative to those mothers without the characteristic, or who do not experience the event. The percentage change can either be positive or negative. A positive percentage change indicates that the effect increases the odds of leaving welfare and causes welfare receipt to be short by increasing the rate of welfare exit for women with the particular attribute or life experience. A negative percentage change indicates that the effect reduces the odds of leaving welfare and slows the speed at which women exit welfare, lengthening receipt for women with that particular attribute.

Table 5.3 presents the results of the event history analysis. Many of the background characteristics shown previously to have a bivariate association with the rate of welfare exit were not important when the effects of changing life circumstances were taken into account in the multivariate analysis. Variables that are not included in the model shown in table 5.3 because they essentially had no independent effect on welfare exits are displayed in table B.9. The fact that background characteristics do not exert significant independent effects on the probability of welfare exit indicates that background factors operate indirectly to affect welfare exits, by influencing the occurrence of intervening life events while the mother is on welfare. For instance, the attribute high educational aspirations does not have a significant direct effect on the probability of welfare exit, but operates indirectly to increase the likelihood of completing high school and obtaining postsecondary education, very important predictors of welfare exits and short spells of receipt (see table 5.3).

Parental welfare receipt is not significant in the exit model, nor does it appear to have much of an indirect effect (see table B.9). This finding supports my claim that parental welfare receipt may operate to increase initial welfare receipt in a mechanical way, by the administrative ease of adding another recipient to a family's welfare grant. However, adolescent mothers whose parents ever received welfare or whose parents were on welfare at the time of pregnancy do not experience greater persistence on welfare than adolescent mothers whose parents did not receive welfare. To the extent that a self-perpetuating welfare culture is defined by the transmission of long-term welfare receipt over the generations, evidence from the Baltimore Study indicates little support for this notion.

Table 5.3   Effects of Background Characteristics and Life Events on the Probability of Welfare Exit

Variable	% Change in Probability of Welfare Exit
High educational aspirations	+6
Married at first birth	+83**
Less than 20 years old	−34
High school education only	+86**
Postsecondary education	+131**
Preschool children present	−42**
Female head	−25
Cumulative years of work experience	+4*
OBRA	+10
Unemployment rate	−10*

*Significant at the .05 level.

**Significant at the .01 level.

Note: See table B.9 for full set of parameter estimates and standard errors.

Marital status at the time of first birth continues to affect welfare transitions. Women who were married at first birth have an 83 percent greater chance of exiting welfare relative to women unmarried at first birth. This effect reflects the relatively brief episodes of welfare experienced by the minority of mothers who were married at first birth. The potential income from a spouse and the presence of an additional caretaker for children reduces the length of welfare spells among married mothers. Mothers who are younger than twenty while they are on welfare end receipt more slowly than the mothers who receive welfare when they are older. Over and above the disadvantaged location of teen-age mothers in their educational, family, and work trajectories whose effects are controlled in the model, teenagers have less human capital, fewer social networks, fewer coping skills, and fewer community and labor market contacts than older women, and these factors probably facilitate more rapid welfare exits as women age.

Related to age, the effects of education, the presence of young children, and work experience are seen in the rest of table 5.3.. Relative to women who drop out of high school, women who complete a high school education increase their odds of welfare exit by 86 percent, and women who go on to obtain some postsecondary education increase their probability of welfare exit by 131 percent. Further education is one strategy that reduces the length of welfare spells. Child care constraints retard welfare exits; the probability of leaving welfare is reduced by 42 percent if the mother has preschool children, compared to the presence of older children. Difficulty with child care arrangements was mentioned frequently by the welfare mothers as reasons for not being able to work or attend school. JoAnn, who quit work when she became pregnant for the second time, cited the lack of child care as the reason for not going back to work after her second child was born. Alice explained that she was not able to return to school after her first child because she and her mother had a falling out and her mother refused to watch her baby.

The accumulation of human capital through work experience helps women leave welfare. With each additional year of job experience, the chances that women exit welfare improve by 4 percent. A final important variable that affects the length of welfare spells is the labor market conditions, measured by the unemployment rate. With each rising point in the unemployment rate, the probability of welfare exit falls by 10 percent, as women's chances of finding work diminish. Note that the implementation of the OBRA legislation increased the exit rates among the Baltimore mothers in the years after the law was passed, but not significantly. Recall that under OBRA working welfare recipients could no longer keep a portion of their labor market earnings, reducing the incentive to combine work and welfare income, and welfare eligibility was severely limited, bumping many recipients off the rolls.

The most important factors that predict welfare exits are those factors that enhance the employability of the young mothers and reduce the obstacles to work—education, work experience, child care constraints, and favorable labor market conditions. Marriage at the time of first birth also increases the likelihood that receipt will be brief. This effect represents more than the presence of a spouse. The absence of a spouse or partner, measured by the female headship variable, does not significantly deter welfare exit. The minority of women who were married at first birth are likely to be selectively different from the women who were not married at conception or did not legitimate a premarital pregnancy. It is likely that these marriages involved more emotional commitment and maturity, and perhaps more support from the families of the teenage parents. Furthermore, early marriage may have enabled mothers to return to school or enter the workforce to supplement the economic security that marriage affords.

Summary

Work and marriage are the main routes by which women exit welfare dependency. Work appears to be the more efficient route off welfare among the Baltimore mothers, as work exits occur more frequently, more rapidly, and seem to be more permanent than marriage or cohabitation exits. Family background and individual characteristics affect welfare exits indirectly by influencing the intervening factors that enhance the work and marriage prospects of welfare mothers. Mothers with more-advantaged family and individual resources are more likely to finish high school, limit their subsequent fertility, obtain work experience, and maintain stable marriages, which increase the likelihood of welfare exit and reduce the length of receipt.

Because work is more important than family structure changes in facilitating welfare exits, the key factors in the process by which women exit welfare dependency are those factors that increase the employability and earnings of welfare mothers. Education, job skills, and few child care constraints increase the probability of finding stable work and leaving welfare. These same factors are likely to enhance the mother's marital prospects as well, especially within the black population (Lichter et al. 1992; South 1991). The impact of family structure changes involving marriage or cohabitation on transitions into and out of welfare dependency seem to operate through the kinds of life course decisions that married and single mothers make about finishing their education, joining the workforce, and having more children.

The finding that work is a major route out of welfare dependency for black inner-city teenage mothers is astounding and has important implications for welfare policies aimed at getting welfare mothers into the labor force. The underlying assumption that welfare mothers do not work or want to work, which drives welfare policies to focus on *making* mothers work, is wrong, and this focus is misplaced. Rather, attention should be directed to the obvious work efforts that are demonstrated by a majority of recipients and the extent to which this work effort is successful in keeping mothers off welfare. This is the topic of the next chapter.

Chapter 6
Welfare Return

Although welfare spells are a short-term phenomena for the majority of teenage mothers, and exits occur more commonly than first thought, maintaining self-sufficiency is often a struggle, and many former welfare recipients return to welfare for continued support. Here is where knowledge of welfare dynamics is lacking. What happens to women when they leave welfare? What are their chances of remaining off welfare, and how do these chances vary across individuals? Are certain routes from welfare more permanent than others? This chapter examines patterns of welfare recycling among the Baltimore mothers and the factors that determine welfare return.

Bane and Ellwood's (1983) and later Ellwood's (1986) pioneering work on welfare dynamics alerted poverty scholars and policymakers to the high rates of "recidivism" that they found, ranging from 34 to over 40 percent. Ellwood (1986) demonstrates that multiple spells of relatively short episodes of welfare receipt transform the portrait of a short-term recipient into a longer-term recipient once the total time on welfare is cumulated (also see Gottschalk and Moffitt 1994). Bane and Ellwood's recent reanalysis (1994) further reports that age, marital status, education, number of children, and work experience have substantial influence on the probability of returning to welfare. Their work, however, measures these factors at the beginning of the first spell of welfare and does not capture the impact of the welfare experience or changing circumstances once women end receipt. Thus, we learn less about the process by which women return to welfare or how some women manage to remain off welfare. In addition, Bane and Ellwood's work reports a greater influence of relationship changes than work activity in precipitating welfare transitions than other studies analyzing monthly data

(Gritz and MaCurdy 1991; Harris 1993; Pavetti 1993; Spalter-Roth and Hartmann 1994a) and than I find among the Baltimore teenage mothers using annual data.

The prevalence of work as a route out of welfare dependency among the Baltimore teenage mothers seems to contradict current notions that welfare mothers have shunned the labor market and refused to participate in work activities (Mead 1986, 1992). The Family Support Act was based on this notion, and the current policy now requires welfare mothers with young children to participate in education, job search, or job training programs. Future welfare reform will likely impose time limits on lifetime receipt, and once limits are reached, welfare mothers would be required to work in mandatory public service jobs to earn their welfare checks. The motivation behind these measures is to socialize mothers to earn their own way and serve as an example to their children, and to get welfare mothers into the paid labor force. Yet, results from the Baltimore data indicate that many recipients have traveled this route. Thus, the policy attention on nonwork is misplaced, and the question remains as to how efficient the work route is in maintaining women's economic independence from welfare.

There is almost no research on what happens to women once they leave welfare, nor is there much knowledge about the work patterns of former welfare recipients.[1] Yet welfare reform and public attention has focused primarily on *getting* women off welfare without much long-range vision for *keeping* them off welfare. This chapter explores these issues by examining the permanency of types of welfare exits and analyzing the factors that cause women to return to welfare. A key segment of the analysis is devoted to identifying the women who successfully maintain a work exit from welfare with important implications for welfare reform policies aimed at moving welfare mothers into the labor force.

Patterns of Welfare Return

Returns to welfare are likely to be associated with the prior welfare experience. In particular, the route by which women leave welfare may affect the longevity of their exit. Work exits are suspected to be highly unstable routes off welfare because such exits do not usually result in large earnings increases. Studies with information on annual income have shown, for instance, that in the year that women exit welfare, more than half report family incomes below the poverty level, and among those who exit through work, 67 percent are poor at the time of exit (Harris 1996). The work that welfare mothers find usually pays low wages without employee benefits and does not offer much promise for advancement (Edin and Lein 1996; Harris 1993; Spalter-Roth and Hartmann, 1994a). The role strains of managing child care, a household, and a job are difficult for middle-class women, let alone poor mothers who lack social support and resources. On the other hand, marriage may not provide a more permanent refuge from welfare. One reason marriage has become a less prevalent route off welfare in the 1980s is its instability, particularly among the low-income population (Mare and Winship 1991).

Table 6.1 presents the cumulative proportion returning to welfare by the type of prior exit for all spells of welfare with observed exits. As in chapter 5, exits are classified according to whether the single mother marries or begins a cohabiting relationship, or whether the mother remains single but either begins to work or works her way off welfare, or whether some other event occurs (in the absence of marriage, cohabitation, and work). The first column of table 6.1 shows the timing of welfare return following all exits. The transition off welfare is most vulnerable soon after welfare exit, as most returns occur within the first three years of leaving welfare. Within two years of leaving welfare, 15 percent of the former welfare mothers have returned for continued support, and another 7 percent return during the third year since exit. The total proportion returning reaches a quarter after four years of ending receipt. The rates of return then begin to drop off, and it takes the rest of the observation period to cumulate another quarter who eventually return. Overall, about half the women who leave welfare return for repeated spells of receipt.[2]

Turning to the patterns of welfare return by type of exit in the remaining columns, marriage or cohabitation exits appear to be the least permanent.[3] Returns occur more rapidly following marriage exits, as 20 percent of the former welfare mothers who left welfare through marriage or cohabitation have returned within two years, compared to 14 percent who left through work and 13 percent who left in other ways. The insecurity of the marriage route continues over time, with higher return rates than the other exit routes at all durations since welfare exit. Work instability occurs during the first four years following a work exit, when about

Table 6.1 The Cumulative Proportion Returning to Welfare by the Type of Welfare Exit

Years Since Welfare Exit	All Exits	Marriage or Cohabitation	Work	Other
1	.08	.14	.06	.11
2	.15	.20	.14	.13
3	.22	.27	.20	.20
4	.26	.31	.25	.24
5	.27	.36	.25	.24
6	.30	.39	.27	.33
7	.32	.41	.32	.37
8	.35	.41	.32	.37
9	.37	.44	.32	.47
10+	.51	.59	.48	.47
N of spells	246	51	154	41

a quarter of the women who left welfare through work return. In the short run, however, those who can maintain their work exit, either through their attachment to the labor force or through supplemental sources of economic support, experience reduced risks of repeat dependency compared to women who exit welfare through marriage.

Women who exit welfare in other ways (e.g., the aging of children, change in residence, or unknown) are most vulnerable to welfare return in the first year following welfare exit, when almost a quarter of the returns following "other" exits occur. Recall that endings that are not associated with observed events are particularly suspect to underreporting of welfare receipt, administrative discovery of unreported labor market earnings, or administrative mistakes and red tape, especially those with short periods of nonreceipt (Ellwood 1986). On the other hand, some of these exits may be related to brief periods in which the mother has obtained income from the father of her children, boyfriends, friends, or family (Edin and Lein 1996; Spalter-Roth and Hartmann 1994b). Such sources are unstable or the level of support fluctuates, causing women to return quickly and often for continued welfare support. Exits associated with relationship changes appear to be the least-promising route to economic security, as 59 percent of women who exit welfare through marriage or cohabitation eventually return to welfare, compared to 48 percent of the women who exit through work and 47 percent of women who exit through some other route.

Return Spell Beginnings

It is tempting to assume that welfare returns following marriage exits occur when marriages fall apart and, similarly, that welfare returns following work exits are due to job instability. Table 6.2 assesses the extent to which the way in which return spells begin is related to the way in which previous spells end. While a relationship between ending and reentry types exists, the variation in reentry types by previous ending type is substantial.

Returns to welfare that follow marriage or cohabitation exits more often occur because of relationship breakup than returns following other exit types. Among all returns, for instance, 12 percent occur because of relationship instability, compared to 21 percent of the returns following marriage exits. Note, however, that nearly half of the returns following marriage exits occur because of job loss and another quarter because of other reasons. Of the returns following work exits, 52 percent occur because of job instability, more than the 47 percent among all returns. However, other events also cause instability in the work route for the former welfare mothers, including marital dissolution, additional childbearing, and probably fluctuations in supplemental income sources. The strongest association between ending and reentry types is found for other reasons. Among returns that follow other endings, 54 percent occur because of other reasons, compared to 34 percent of all returns overall. The fairly strong correlation between the other ending and beginning types

Table 6.2   Percent Distribution of Return Spell Beginnings by Type of Previous Spell Ending

| | **Previous Ending Type** | | | |
Return Type	**Marriage or Cohabitation**	**Work**	**Other**	**All Endings**
Marital/cohab breakup	20.8	9.3	7.7	12.1
Job loss	45.8	51.9	30.8	47.3
Additional birth	8.3	5.6	7.7	6.6
Other	25.0	33.3	53.9	34.1
Total %	100.0	100.0	100.0	100.0
N of spells	24	54	13	91

suggests that these spell endings and return beginnings could be due to administrative churning. If a mother is bumped off welfare, she can only be returned to welfare through administrative mechanisms. However, the same correlation could result if these transitions were due to fluctuating income flows from family and friends.

Although the association between the causes of welfare exit and welfare return is evident, the fact that there is substantial variation in the causes that precipitate welfare return by each of the exit types indicates the dynamic nature of young mothers' lives and the numerous economic strategies that welfare mothers employ to leave welfare dependency and to maintain their welfare exits. Multiple strategies may be necessary to remain off welfare. Many mothers who exit through marriage or cohabitation later enter the labor market to increase their economic security. When they lose their jobs, their families are at risk to welfare return. Despite working, former welfare mothers whose marriages fail also face the likelihood of repeat dependency. And women who exit welfare in other ways may eventually enter the workforce to supplement and add stability to the income sources at hand. Note that overall the most common reason for welfare return is job loss. To supplement additional sources of income from a spouse, a partner, family, friends, a boyfriend, or the absent father, or in the absence of these sources, the mother's earning ability and labor market success is crucial. Because women are at risk to welfare return later in their life course as parents, following initial welfare receipt, repeat dependency seems to be more related to the mother's work activities than to the family events involving marriage and childbearing.

The case history of a cycling recipient, JoAnn, illustrates this theme. JoAnn spent her first spell on welfare while she was married and did not work. Her marriage dissolved while she was still on welfare, but she soon began a new relationship. When she and her boyfriend decided to cohabit together, JoAnn left welfare. Soon after that, she began to work. With income from her job and the security of her relationship, she remained off welfare for five years. She married her partner, but lost her job the following year. Even though JoAnn was still married, the loss of her income meant the family had to return to welfare. Soon after, her second marriage began to falter, and she separated and remained on welfare. Her second spell lasted for six years, which ended when JoAnn found a job in 1984.

JoAnn's story is one of marital instability, but it emphasizes the point that one source of income is often not enough. Even when she was married and her husband worked as a laborer, JoAnn often waitressed at a local coffee shop to improve their family's economic circumstances. Movement off welfare involves replacing welfare income with some other source of income, either from a spouse or partner, from the mother's own labor market earnings, or from family and friends. Most of the Baltimore mothers' income packages included multiple sources, and loss of any supplemental source increased their risks of welfare return.

Differential Rates of Return

With a better understanding of some of the circumstances surrounding welfare return, I now turn to examine the influence of background and individual characteristics on rates of welfare return. A priori, we might expect background characteristics to have less of an influence at this later stage of the mother's life course than during initial welfare entry, as events and life circumstances have intervened to shape the young mother's life situation. However, to the extent that background and individual characteristics are related to the mother's earning ability and labor market success, certain characteristics may differentiate the speed at which mothers return to the welfare program following previous receipt, given that work loss is a common cause of repeat receipt.

Figure 6.1 shows the percent of former welfare mothers who return for a repeat spell of welfare within two years of the prior exit by family background characteristics and by individual attributes at the time of pregnancy or first birth. As expected, family background factors hardly differentiate rates of return (see 6.1A). There are no differences by parental education or whether the mother was also a teen mother, and family structure in adolescence exerts an effect opposite to what one would expect. Former welfare mothers who grew up with two parents were more likely to return to welfare rapidly than the mothers who lived in a one-parent home. Only parental welfare receipt differentiates the speed at which mothers return to welfare, but the differences are not significant. Among those mothers whose parents received welfare, 19 percent of former welfare mothers return for multiple spells within two years of ending prior receipt, compared to 12 percent among the mothers whose parents were never on welfare.

101

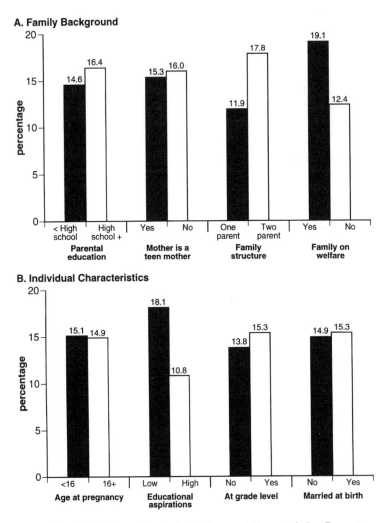

Figure 6.1 Rapid Return Entries by Background Characteristics: Percent Returning to Welfare within Two Years of Previous Exit.

Similar results are shown in figure 6.1B. The age at pregnancy, marital status at first birth, and on-time progression through school reveal no differences in return rates among former welfare mothers. Only educational aspirations differentiate return rates; adolescents who expressed aspirations to obtain a postsecondary education were less likely to return to welfare rapidly than adolescents who expressed lower aspirations. Apparently, background characteristics do not even exert indirect effects on the probability of welfare return by influencing other factors that affect rates of return, such as education, the tempo of childbearing, and labor market attachment. To the extent that background factors influence these intervening life events, differences in the bivariate analysis would appear (see fig. 6.1). Rather, the circumstances at the time of welfare exit and the intermediate life events that occur since the exit are likely to impact more urgently on the probability of welfare return.

The Determinants of Welfare Return

Given that the most vulnerable time of welfare return is soon after welfare exit, factors related to the work and marriage routes off welfare are likely to play an important role in the determinants of welfare return. The process by which women return to welfare is therefore modeled as a function of age and child care constraints at the time of welfare exit, the accumulation of human capital, headship status, labor market conditions, and job and marital stability since welfare exit. Using event history methods, three separate models of welfare return are estimated (see table 6.3). The determinants of welfare return following all exits are shown in the first column. Models of welfare return by the route of exit are shown in the second and third columns, contrasting the work route with all other exit routes (combining the marriage or cohabitation route with the other routes off welfare). Effects are presented as the percentage change in the probability of returning to welfare for mothers with a given characteristic or who experience a certain life event relative to women without the given characteristic or who do not experience the certain life event.

Focusing on the overall return model in the first column, a large family size, female headship, and the events of job loss and marital or relationship dissolution are the important predictors of welfare return. Women who have three or more children at the time of welfare exit have a 37 percent greater likelihood of returning to welfare than women with

Table 6.3 Determinants of the Probability of Welfare Return by Exit Route

| | % Change in Probability of Welfare Return | | |
	All Exits	**Work Exit**	**Marital/Cohab & Other Exit**
At welfare exit:			
less than 20 years old	+13	+16	+20
3 or more children	+37**	+72**	+1
High school education only	−31	−17	−42
Post-secondary education	−29	−36	+7
Female head of household	+86**	+116**	+71
Marital/cohabitaion breakup	+93**	+68	+116*
Job loss	+276**	+384**	+233**
Unemployment rate	+5	−2	+16

*Significant at .05 level.

**Significant at .05 level.

Note: See table B.12 for full set of parameter estimates and standard errors.

fewer children. Providing for a large family imposes economic strains on all parents and must be especially difficult for poor women who just left welfare, especially if the woman is unmarried and relying on her own labor market earnings. Former welfare mothers who maintain their own households with no other adults present remain at high risk to welfare return, probably because they have fewer supplemental sources of income and fewer social supports and available caretakers for children. Women who are female heads of household face an 86 percent higher probability of welfare return relative to married women or women who live with other adults or family members.

Surprisingly, the accumulation of human capital captured in the effects of age and education are not significant predictors of welfare return in any model. While education helps women leave welfare, it does not seem to be as important in maintaining welfare exits as the sudden instability of relationships and jobs.[4] Women who experience marital or cohabitation dissolution increase their probability of welfare return by 93 percent, compared to women who do not experience relationship instability.[5] The most potent predictor of welfare return is job loss. The probability of repeat dependence on welfare increases by almost 300 percent when women lose their jobs.

When we examine the process of welfare return by the route of exit, interesting differences emerge. Child care constraints, female headship, and job instability determine welfare returns among the women who exit welfare through work, while job and marital instability cause the women who left welfare through marriage or other routes to return for multiple spells. Clearly, arranging child care for many children, a single source of income, lack of social support, and unstable employment make the work route especially difficult to maintain for former welfare mothers. The greater number of children require more complex child care arrangements and increase the costs of care (Presser and Baldwin 1980). With a wider age range, children are likely to need different kinds of child care settings depending on their age, increasing the likelihood that any one arrangement will be unstable over time. When child care arrangements fall through, mothers cannot work and usually lose their jobs since low-wage workers are easily replaced. Many mothers quit work because the conflicts and hassles are too much for them to handle (see Edin and Lein 1996).

This situation becomes especially acute for female heads, who lack the social supports and emergency help with child care that a spouse, partner, or additional adults or family members may offer. As a huge literature has documented for middle-class working mothers (see Moen 1992 for a review), labor market continuity depends on stable child care arrangements and social support systems, and these factors are especially instrumental for poor mothers who are struggling to maintain their work exits from welfare, most working at minimum wages. One reason JoAnn, the case study of a cycling recipient, did not work during the six years following her first birth was because of the demands of caring for two young children and the lack of affordable child care. When JoAnn left welfare for the second time in 1984, she was a female head of household and worked as a cashier for $3.65 an hour. Her children were in their teens, which helped solve the child care problem, but she still had to pay for transportation expenses and work clothes. In 1984, her first year off welfare through work, JoAnn did not have a savings account, a checking account, a credit card, or a driver's license.

Among the women who exit through marriage, cohabitation, or other routes, the loss of income sources primarily propel them back on to welfare (see column three, table 6.3). If the marriage that facilitated welfare exit splits up, the probability of welfare return increases by 233 percent. Women who exit in other ways may eventually marry or cohabit but return to welfare if the relationship does not remain stable.

As we saw earlier, many women who exit welfare through marriage or other routes eventually enter the labor market to increase the security of their economic situation (see table 6.2). When they lose this additional source of income, their chances of welfare return increase by 116 percent. Again, I find evidence that multiple sources of income are necessary for former welfare mothers to maintain their welfare exits, consistent with other studies of welfare mothers (see Harris 1996; Spalter-Roth and Hartmann 1994b). The labor market earnings of female heads are not sufficient to maintain work exits because most work at minimum-wage jobs with no employee benefits. Marriage is usually not sufficient to maintain marriage exits, and most mothers eventually enter the job market. Although marriage affords some economic security, it is not a mechanism for social mobility among welfare mothers. Women who exit in other ways either marry or begin to work to help keep them off welfare and supplement their meager and disparate sources of income. When these additional sources of income through marriage or the workforce are lost, women and their families are likely to return to welfare for continuing economic support.

Summary

Women are most vulnerable to welfare return soon after leaving welfare, when job instability is high and women are adjusting to a new marriage or are counting on income flows from others. Half of all the women who return to welfare do so within four years of leaving. The longer a woman is able to maintain her welfare exit, the less likely she is to return. The most important factors that help women sustain their welfare exits are those factors that enable women to maintain stable employment, including a small family size and the social support of other adults, family, or partners with whom the mother lives.

Marriage or cohabitation exits appear to be less permanent than work and other exits. Part of the insecurity of relationship exits is the high rate of instability in marriages and cohabitation among the young and the poor (Cherlin 1992). But another part involves a choice that young women may make to direct their energies and activities toward their family and domestic role, putting aside for the moment their education or work career. When marriages and cohabitation falter, young mothers may face the prospects of providing for themselves and their children with less education, less-recent work experience, and more children than the women who pursued an education and early work role. These additional burdens may hasten the return to welfare for mothers who try to enter the world of work after marital dissolution.

Among the three types of welfare recipients in the Baltimore Study, cyclers are characterized by early marriage, high school dropout, and rapid subsequent fertility, reflecting the choice of a family route over the education route soon after becoming teenage mothers. If marriages fall apart, and over two-thirds of the early marriages of the Baltimore mothers did (Furstenberg, Brooks-Gunn, and Morgan 1987), these early circumstances may put into motion a cycling pattern of work and welfare, where work is particularly unstable because of the consequences associated with early life course decisions. Instability describes the life course of the cycling women.

The predominance of work in the lives of welfare mothers is again evident from the analysis in this chapter. Even among the women who exited welfare through marriage or other routes, many eventually entered the labor force. We know this because job loss is the most frequent event occurring at the time of reentry and is a major determinant of welfare return among all types of welfare exits. Women enter the labor market to supplement income from a partner or from family and friends, or women may begin to work when their relationships dissolve. Women who exit through work may also marry, though marriage is less common along the work route off welfare than work is along the marriage route. These results indicate that work or marriage alone is not sufficient to keep women off welfare.

As a result, the route by which women exit welfare has less of an impact on the longevity of their welfare exit than do the unfolding life events and circumstances that occur after the exit. As life circumstances change, young mothers constantly adjust their economic strategies to pool multiple sources of income into a package that can sustain their families and enable them to stay off welfare. Most of these strategies involve work at some point in time. When any one source is lost to the income package, mothers are likely to return to welfare until they can develop a new strategy to replace or regain the lost income source.

Chapter 7
Work and Welfare

In the recent literature on urban poverty, labor force participation has been given an especially prominent place (e.g., Freeman 1991; Kasarda 1989; Levitan and Shapiro 1987; Mead 1992; Tienda and Stier 1991; Wilson 1987). Concern over declining work activity among the urban poor has generated ongoing debates as to the explanations for nonwork and solutions to encourage work and reduce welfare dependency. A structural perspective argues that in addition to their disadvantaged abilities and skills to obtain stable jobs and decent wages, the urban poor are further constrained by a lack of opportunities as a result of the industrial transformations of the inner city and social and residential isolation (Massey and Denton 1989, 1993; Wacquant and Wilson 1989; Wilson 1987). The cultural perspective claims that the poor reject the menial, minimum-wage jobs that are available in the inner cities; so nonwork is viewed as both the inability to obtain a job and an unwillingness to even look for one (Kaus 1986; Mead 1986, 1992; Murray 1984). Regardless of the explanation for the diminished work efforts of the urban poor, most people agree that this is not a good situation and that work should be encouraged, or even enforced, as an essential aspect of American family life.

This theme has occupied the recent welfare reform debates as well, and at the heart of these debates is the issue of work disincentives. For instance, the current welfare system undermines work activity among recipients. When welfare recipients work, they lose a dollar in benefits for each dollar earned, leaving a woman economically no better off if she is employed.[1] If her earnings rise above the maximum AFDC grant, which averages about 40 percent of the poverty line, then she is ineligible for cash assistance and loses health care benefits as well (U.S. House of Representatives 1994). Thus, welfare mothers who work but remain poor risk worsening their situation. On the other hand, as an entitlement program, welfare cash assistance is guaranteed to those in poverty without any societal obligations in return (Gilder 1981; Mead 1986; Murray 1984). It therefore appears that our welfare policies discourage work and send the wrong message to the poor about individual responsibility in the economic support of children. Rising public anxiety over the relationship between work and welfare has prompted policymakers to call for an end to welfare as an entitlement and for more stringent work obligations on those who do receive benefits.

Notions about nonwork and the lack of work effort among the poor are not consistent with the findings in this study. Work is the most common route of welfare exit for the Baltimore mothers, and job loss is the main reason women return. The prevalence of work in the lives of teenage mothers on welfare is a rather surprising finding. Teenage mothers are often limited by a lack of education, work experience, job skills, and access to child care—factors that certainly affect work transitions and careers. Rather than restricting young mothers from ever working, however, these factors may define the type and quality of work teen mothers can obtain, and this may have more important implications for the length and patterns of welfare receipt than the mothers' work efforts. This chapter explores these issues in depth by examining the relationship between work and welfare among the Baltimore mothers over the twenty years following their first birth.

Work and Welfare

Surprisingly little research has been done on the relationship between work and welfare, yet it is widely assumed that any adult with a job does not need welfare assistance. Employment is equated with economic self-sufficiency. Such assumptions motivated the 1988 Family Support Act, emphasizing job training and work requirements for recipients. This policy is based on the premise that the opportunity to work and contact with the labor market will increase job skills and work experience, as well as self-esteem and sense of achievement (Cottingham and Ellwood 1989; Ellwood 1988). As a result, recipients become less isolated from mainstream society, and their earnings, or at least their potential for earnings, should increase, enabling them to leave welfare dependency and rely solely on their labor market income.

Concern that the existence of an income support system discourages work among the poor seems warranted by social science research. Among the studies that examine the effects of welfare policies on the behavior of the poor, the only consistent and significant findings suggest a negative impact on labor supply (see Duncan and Hoffman 1988; Moffitt 1992). Although the estimates vary, a review of the evidence suggests that AFDC reduces the average work effort among single mothers on welfare by about 5.4 hours a week (Danziger, Haveman, and Weinberg 1981), which Moffitt (1992) estimates would result in about a one-thousand-dollar reduction in the annual earnings of female heads (in 1989), an amount that is unlikely to affect their poverty rates. Moffitt (1983, 1992) also finds that work disincentives in the welfare program mainly affect work effort and do not appear to have a large impact on AFDC participation. That is, the existence of the welfare program does not cause women to quit work in order to receive AFDC benefits, but women who are on welfare work less. However, much of the policy debate has missed the evidence showing the degree to which welfare mothers do participate in the labor force (Duncan 1984; Garfinkel and McLanahan 1986; Harrison 1977; Jencks 1991; Levitan and Shapiro 1987; Pearce 1979, 1983; Rein and Rainwater 1978; Tienda 1990), and the strong desire to work expressed by the poor (Goodwin 1983; Tienda and Stier 1991).

The first policy initiative to encourage work among welfare recipients was established in 1967 when recipients were allowed to keep a portion of their earnings when they worked, without having them deducted from their benefits.[2] Work incentives were built into the system in the hopes of moving recipients off welfare and onto the payrolls. Although numerous programs to encourage work have been implemented since 1967, welfare-to-work programs have been largely unsuccessful in the past because they typically had scarce resources and lacked effective coordination between employment and welfare offices (Bane and Ellwood 1994). Those who obtained work through the programs were primarily placed in low-wage jobs that do not improve job skills or sufficiently support a family, and any modest gains in income among the program participants occurred because of increases in work hours, not wage rates (Blank 1994; Block et al. 1987; Goodwin 1983; Pearce 1979). Thus, program-related jobs may get mothers more readily into the workforce or increase the work hours of low-wage workers, but they do not provide much long-range promise for becoming independent of an income support program. Moving from welfare to self-sufficiency through work, then, should be highly dependent on recipients' resources and abilities to find stable employment that pays a living wage.

Although recent studies have reported a greater degree of work activity among welfare mothers than was previously thought, the evidence shows that women who are at risk to long-term welfare dependence are those women who face lower probabilities of success in the job market. This body of research again targets the group of teenage mothers in the Baltimore Study. Young, single, black mothers with many children, without a high school education, or without previous earnings or job skills are prone to persistent welfare dependency because of their deficiencies in the job market (Bane and Ellwood 1983; Duncan 1984; Ellwood 1986; O'Neill, Bassi, and Wolf 1987; O'Neill et al. 1984). Furthermore, women living in the inner cities are more likely to experience chronic dependence on welfare and labor market detachment in the context of social isolation from mainstream institutions (McLanahan and Garfinkel 1989; Reischauer 1989; Wacquant and Wilson 1989).

This chapter examines the process by which the Baltimore mothers work their way off welfare. The relationship between labor market experience and welfare dependency is analyzed by examining the transition into the labor force and the ways in which work provides a route out of dependency for the young mothers. The analysis focuses particularly on welfare exits through work that are subgrouped into job exits, when the woman begins to work and leaves welfare, and work exits, when the woman works her way off welfare through cumulative work experience.

To explain the process of working off welfare through either a job exit or a work exit, two transitions are analyzed. First, I examine the transition to work among women on welfare and whether entry into the labor market results in an exit from welfare. By dichotomizing work transitions into whether or not work entry coincides with welfare exit, I can contrast the determinants of these work transitions to better understand how labor market behavior is related to welfare behavior. This analysis allows me to describe those women who find a job that lifts them out of welfare and those women who find work but remain dependent on welfare.

Among those women who do not leave welfare when they begin to work, I then analyze their transition off welfare. Do they eventually work their way off welfare through work experience or do other life course factors such as marriage, family size, or education determine their length of welfare receipt?

Combining Work and Welfare

Working women and married women were eligible for welfare in the state of Maryland if total family income was below the break-even income (eligibility cut-off).[3] The policy changes in the Omnibus Budget Reconciliation Act of 1981 largely affected working welfare mothers by reducing the incentives to work while on welfare. Because OBRA increased the rate at which benefits are reduced when earnings increase, women who could not earn enough income to leave welfare had less to gain economically from work (see Bane and Ellwood 1994, 153). Balanced against the costs involved with child care and loss of time with children, the lack of a gain in income made work while on welfare less practical, and the percentage of recipients who reported labor market earnings in census and caseload data dropped after OBRA was implemented (Jencks 1991, 59; Moffitt 1992). This legislation affected the Baltimore mothers who combined work and welfare income after 1981, when most of the mothers were in their early thirties. Therefore, the level of earned income was the main factor that might preclude mothers from welfare eligibility throughout the study period.

Figure 7.1 shows the extent to which the Baltimore mothers supplemented welfare income with labor market income. The percentage of recipients who also reported working while on welfare is shown at various points during the study period in figure 7.1A and for varying lengths of receipt in figure 7.1B. At the time of the first teenage birth, it is understandable that a large proportion of the mothers who were receiving welfare were dependent on its income as their primary means of support (only 17.9 percent were also working). However, over time, as the young mothers finished school, raised their children, and accumulated work experience, they were more likely to work, and in many cases, combined work and welfare income to support their families. In any given year during the study, about one-quarter of the Baltimore mothers were receiv-

A. Percent of Recipients also Working by Selected Calendar Years

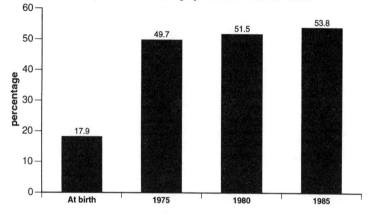

B. Percent of Recipients also Working by Cumulative Years of Receipt

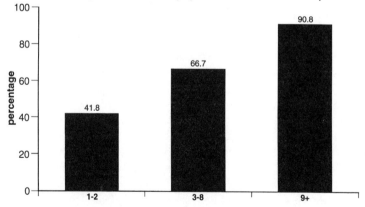

Figure 7.1   The Incidence of Work While Receiving Welfare

ing welfare, and about half of them were also working. Selected years are shown in figure 7.1A.

The more extensive welfare use is within the study period, the more likely welfare income is supplemented by income from a job. Recipients who experience the most persistent dependency are much more likely to simultaneously work during welfare receipt than recipients who have brief stays on welfare. Figure 7.1B shows that about two-fifths of the women who received welfare for one or two years were also working; while practically all (91 percent) of the women who experienced nine or more years of welfare support supplemented this income with labor market earnings.

These data indicate that welfare recipients most at risk to long-term dependency are far from detached from the labor market. Moreover, there does not seem to be much support for the idea that welfare receipt fosters a type of behavioral dependency that rejects the mainstream value placed on work (Mead 1986; Murray 1984). The more persistent welfare receipt is, the greater the likelihood of labor force participation. The critical question, however, is whether work provides an efficient route out of welfare dependency.

Routes of Exit through Work

There are two ways women can leave welfare through work. Young mothers can rely on welfare without working, then find a job and leave welfare. I refer to these work exits as "new job" exits. Other women can combine work and welfare, as nearly half do each year, and continue to work until they leave welfare. These work exits are referred to as "work off welfare" exits. Recall that work exits occur in the absence of relationship changes and causes of ineligibility (e.g., children aging). When work exits are subgrouped this way, about half of the 63 percent of work exits overall occur when the mother begins to work and leaves welfare. The remaining half represent work off welfare exits, when the mother combines work and welfare until she eventually exits.

The speed at which spells of welfare end by these two work exit types is examined in table 7.1. The cumulative percentage of those exiting welfare by duration of receipt is shown by the type of exit for initial and return spells. The distributions in the total columns illustrate again that spells end rather quickly. About half of all spells end after two years,

48.7 percent of initial spells and 55.2 percent of return spells last for two years. Beyond two years of receipt, the rates of welfare exit decline so that 25 percent of the teenage mothers remain in their first spell of welfare for ten years or more.

The rates of leaving welfare by type of exit differ in initial and return spells. In initial spells, job exits occur more rapidly than work off exits; however, return spells end more quickly through work experience than through labor market entry. After two years of receipt, 18.7 percent of all initial spells end when the mother finds a new job; 11.8 percent end when the mother works her way off welfare; and 18.2 percent end in other ways, including marriage, cohabitation, and receipt of income from other sources. In contrast, after two years in a return spell, 15.0 percent of all women exit through a new job, while 18.3 percent exit through labor market attachment.

Table 7.1 Cumulative Percent of Women Exiting Welfare by Duration of Receipt and Type of Exit for Initial and Return Spells

Duration (Years)	New job	Work off welfare	Other	Total
Initial Spell (N = 204)				
1	12.3	8.4	11.3	31.9
2	18.7	11.8	18.2	48.7
3	21.2	14.8	19.7	55.6
4	22.1	15.3	21.2	58.6
5	22.6	18.2	21.7	62.5
6	23.2	19.8	22.2	65.1
7	23.7	20.3	23.7	67.6
8	24.7	20.3	24.7	69.7
9	26.2	21.8	24.7	72.8
10	26.7	21.8	26.8	75.3
11	27.3	22.3	26.8	76.4
12	27.3	22.9	28.5	78.6
13	29.6	24.0	29.0	82.6
14	30.1	24.0	30.2	84.3
15+	30.1	29.4	33.9	93.4
Return Spell (N = 91)				
1	9.0	13.6	14.7	37.3
2	15.0	18.3	21.9	55.2
3	15.0	19.7	24.5	59.2
4	18.2	22.8	30.8	71.7
5	20.1	24.7	32.7	77.6
6+	29.1	24.7	36.3	90.1

In initial spells, job exits occur more rapidly and earlier in the spell, while exits through labor market experience occur more slowly and later, so that over time, about an equal proportion of women exit through these two routes. Among women who return to welfare, however, contact with the labor market during receipt improves the likelihood that they will quickly exit welfare again. Initial spells are more likely to end through a new job when women are younger and many are possibly still finishing their education. Return spells occur later in the young mother's life, on average, after most women have obtained some work experience. As we saw in chapter 6, return spells are commonly due to job instability; women who lose their jobs or must cut back on their hours find themselves back on welfare. Many repeat recipients find work again or continue to work until they eventually work their way off welfare through cumulative work experience.

Other exit routes that involve primarily marriage, residential changes, additional income flows from family or friends, or when children age also occur fairly rapidly, especially in return spells of welfare. However, relative to the overall work route (combining new job and work off welfare exits), marriage and other routes occur less frequently and are less permanent.

The case histories of an early-exit and cycling recipient fit these patterns. Chandra relied on welfare for two years after her first child was born in 1967 so that she could finish her high school education. Occasionally, Chandra worked part-time at a local cleaners, but for the most part, Chandra did not work while she was in school. In 1969 Chandra obtained her high school diploma and got a job as a typist working forty hours a week, at an hourly wage of $1.40. She heard about the job from the local neighborhood youth corps training center. Chandra never returned to welfare. She continued to gain job skills and worked in every subsequent year of the study, despite getting married in 1971.

JoAnn did not work in her first spell on welfare, which ended with a relationship change. She did work while she was off welfare, but lost her job and returned to welfare when she began to experience problems in her marriage. Through her previous contact with the labor force, she was able to land another job as a cashier at a food service store at the nearby shopping center, though it did not provide enough income for JoAnn to leave welfare. She combined her job income with welfare income for two years until 1986 when her hourly wage reached $5.00 and she left welfare.

In sum, there appear to be two results to the work transition among women on welfare. One group of women finds work, and it moves them off welfare. Another group finds work, but it does not provide sufficient wages or hours to move them off welfare. The latter group continues working on welfare until they either increase their hours or increase their wages by gaining a promotion or finding a better paying job. The next set of analyses further explores these two processes of exiting welfare through work.

The Transition to Work

When women on welfare enter the labor force, their earnings determine whether they are still eligible for welfare. If job income exceeds the welfare eligibility cutoff, they move off AFDC. Clearly, the type of job they obtain determines their movement from welfare. Unfortunately, the Baltimore data do not provide information about occupation, wages, or hours on a yearly basis to complement the job histories. However, we can indirectly assess the type of work women are likely to obtain by examining the characteristics of the young mothers on welfare who also work.

Background characteristics of the young mother relate to her parental family and represent some measure of her relative disadvantage in family resources. Individual characteristics of the teenager during pregnancy or at the time of first birth may also affect her ability to gain employment. Age, high educational aspirations, and good school performance should enhance a mother's job prospects by increasing the likelihood that she finishes high school and possibly obtains further training. The life circumstances of the young mother at welfare entry and labor market entry may differentiate those women who find a job that results in welfare exit from those who do not leave welfare when they begin to work. Older, educated, or married teen mothers possess additional resources in the form of maturity, training, skills, or potential earnings, which should improve the probability that work will result in welfare exit. On the other hand, a large family may impede the completion of education or other types of training, as well as impose child care constraints thereby lowering the chances that mothers with many children will find work with pay and benefits adequate for them to leave welfare.

Table 7.2 presents the mean characteristics of the welfare mothers

Table 7.2 Characteristics of Recipients Who Begin to Work by Whether the Transition to Work Results in Welfare Exit, Means, or Mean Proportions

	Work & Still On Welfare (N = 106)[1]	Work & Welfare Exit (N = 70)[1]
Family background:		
Parental education high school or more	0.18	0.28
Mother has 4+ siblings	0.69	0.75
Parents received welfare*	0.37	0.20
Single-parent household at pregnancy	0.41	0.33
Individual characteristics:		
<16 at pregnancy*	0.41	0.23
High educational aspirations	0.35	0.39
At grade level in school	0.70	0.76
At beginning of welfare spell:		
Age	18.3	19.5
3 or more children	0.10	0.11
Preschool children present	0.92	0.84
Graduated high school*	0.12	0.33
Married	0.28	0.29
Year of entry into labor force:		
Age	23.3	23.0
3 or more children	0.27	0.16
Preschool children present	0.25	0.21
Graduated high school*	0.33	0.54
On welfare 5 years or more before beginning to work*	0.34	0.20

*Differences statistically significant at the .05 level.

[1]N = number of work transitions among women on welfare.

who begin to work by whether the transition to work results in an exit from welfare. In general, women who have a more-advantaged family background, were older at first pregnancy, have smaller families, and finish high school are more likely to leave welfare when they enter the labor market than younger women with fewer family resources, more children, and less human capital. The differences in family background show that recipients who enter the labor force but remain on welfare are more likely to come from single-parent households and to have parents who are less educated and who had also received welfare than the recipients who leave welfare once they begin to work. For instance, 37 percent of the women who work yet continue on welfare grew up in a welfare family, compared to 20 percent of the women who exit welfare when they find a job.

Age, in particular, differentiates those who exit through a job and those who do not. A young age at pregnancy seems to set in motion a chain of events that leads to a more disadvantaged sequence of work and welfare. Mothers who remain dependent on welfare, even though they work, were younger at first pregnancy, entered welfare younger, and began to work later than mothers who exit welfare. Therefore, the women who combine work and welfare experience longer periods of welfare receipt since they are dependent for a longer time before they enter the labor force, and they continue to receive welfare once they are working.

Differences in education and family size also help explain the more persistent dependency associated with the process of combining work and welfare. Although many of the young mothers rely on welfare while they finish high school, indicated by the increasing proportions of high school graduates from the point of welfare entry to the point of labor market entry, the women who find work and leave welfare hold an educational advantage over those whose work is unable to move them out of welfare. In addition, women who must combine work with welfare are further disadvantaged by subsequent births while on welfare, perhaps prompting the need to work to support their families.

The profiles of these two groups of women support a human capital perspective of labor market entry. The women who exit welfare when they find work are those with family and educational resources who are most likely to secure the higher-quality jobs. The women who do not leave welfare when they begin to work come from more disadvantaged families, have less education, and more children to support. Child care constraints may limit the hours the mother can work, or deficiencies in education and family resources may force her into low-wage employment. And part-time or low-wage employment does not move women off welfare. Although only a few of the differences reported in table 7.2 are significant, the most consistent and powerful discriminator is education, which clearly determines who gets the better-paying jobs that lead to welfare exit.

Differences in table 7.2, however, are measured at a point in time. Over the course of a welfare spell, the mother's life circumstances may change and the likelihood of finding a good-paying job may change along with other events. Graduating high school, having another child, or moving in with a partner are dynamic events that continuously affect the probability of finding work and leaving welfare. Moreover, the likelihood of changing life course events such as education and fertility are influenced by family background and individual characteristics. Therefore, a dynamic analysis is needed to test for the independent effects of these factors in determining the transition to work by whether work results in welfare exit.

When Work Helps Women Exit Welfare

Using event history methods, I now examine the effects of changing life circumstances on the probability of entering the labor market by whether the work transition results in welfare exit. The life events I examine include graduating high school, subsequent childbearing, and entering marriage or a cohabiting relationship. Completing high school should improve the woman's chances of obtaining a good job and leaving welfare by increasing the wage she can command with better skills and training. In contrast, it is expected that the more children a welfare mother has, the less likely she is to work, or if she does enter the labor market, the less likely her work will result in welfare exit.

Marriage or cohabitation may have a negative effect on the transition to work among welfare mothers since the need for additional income may be reduced. On the other hand, another adult in the household may relieve the mother of child care responsibilities and increase her likelihood of work. Marriage may also select women who are successful in the work domain as well, a characteristic that likely increased their marriageability (Lichter et al. 1992; South 1991). In this scenario, marriage is expected to increase the likelihood of work that expedites welfare exit.

In addition to changing life circumstances, prior work experience, labor market conditions and welfare policy parameters will affect the probability of work among welfare mothers and the chance that such work will move women off welfare. Previous contact with the labor force is expected to have a positive influence on the transition to work among welfare mothers by improving job skills, enhancing self-esteem, and increasing information networks (Cottingham and Ellwood 1989; Ellwood 1988). An increase in the unemployment rate should deter women from exiting welfare through a job and make it more difficult to supplement welfare income with earnings. Finally, the impact of the OBRA legislation passed in 1981 reduced the incentives to work among women on welfare.

Table 7.3 Determinants of the Transition to Work by Whether Work Results in Welfare Exit

Variable	% Change in Probability of Work		
	Work & Exit	Work & No Exit	Work & Exit vs. Work & No Exit
Parents received welfare	−27	+45	−50
< 16 at first pregnancy	−29	+13	−37
High educational aspirations	−18	+25	−34
At grade level	+82	+46	+25
At spell beginning:			
married	+31	+28	+2
in school	+92	−7	+105
Previous work experience	−76*	−12	−72*
Graduate high school	+186*	+27	+125*
3 or more children	−65*	−52*	−27
Marry or cohabit	+70	+99	+239*
Age	+13*	+5	+7
OBRA	−21	−21	−.1
Rise in unemployment	−24	−16	−9

*Significant at .05 level

Note: See table B.13 for full set of parameter estimates and standard errors.

The results in table 7.3 indicate which factors are important in differentiating three groups of welfare mothers: those who work and exit, those who work and do not exit, and those who do not work. The first column contrasts those who work and exit with those who do not work; the second column contrasts those who work but remain on welfare with those who do not work. The third column then contrasts women who start to work and exit welfare with women who start to work but remain on welfare. Findings from the first contrast indicate that mothers who graduate high school, have fewer than three children, and have no previous work experience are more likely to work and leave welfare than to rely on welfare income alone. Age is also an advantage in landing a job that provides enough income security or fringe benefits to leave welfare. The distinguishing factor in the second contrast between mothers who combine work and welfare and mothers who do not work is family size. Welfare mothers with three or more children are significantly less likely to work than mothers with fewer children.

Results from the third contrast reveal the factors that determine whether labor market entry results in welfare exit and are the primary focus of this analysis. Family background and individual characteristics are not very powerful discriminators of these two groups of welfare mothers. Across all contrasts, family and individual characteristics have either insignificant or indirect effects in predicting the various groups of welfare mothers.

Education, marriage, and previous work experience determine who leaves welfare through a new job and who does not. Family size is only important in distinguishing work status among welfare mothers, rather than differentiating welfare exits among women who work. Therefore, the presence of many children prolongs welfare dependency by making it more difficult for women to work. Women who marry or move in with a partner are more likely to exit welfare when they work than women who work but remain female household heads. Undoubtedly, two adults making arrangements for children when women work is easier than one. But more importantly, we find evidence once again indicating that work or marriage alone is not sufficient to move women off welfare. The fact that working single mothers are still eligible for welfare speaks to the economic insecurity of their jobs.

Education again proves to be an important distinguishing factor as to whether work moves women off welfare. More-educated mothers obtain the better-paying jobs that lead to economic independence from welfare. The surprising result, however, is the effect for previous work experience. Previous work experience actually *retards* welfare exit and describes the more disadvantaged women on welfare who work, but work either fewer hours or at low-paying jobs.

These results suggest that teenage mothers who substitute work for education experience more persistence on welfare. That is, teenage mothers who rely on welfare while they finish their high school education are choosing a more efficient route to economic independence than teens who drop out of school and enter the labor market prematurely, with few skills and no training.

This finding is illustrated by the early life course decisions of Chandra, the early-exit recipient, and Alice, the persistent recipient. At the time of the first birth, Chandra relied on welfare and returned to school, putting off full-time work until she finished her high school degree two years later. In contrast, Alice entered welfare the same year as her first birth, at the age of fifteen. She quit school but also began to work in the same year that she entered welfare. She remained on welfare for fifteen years, and she worked for thirteen of her fifteen years on welfare. By 1978 she was working in her fourth job as a cloth spreader in a men's clothing manufacturing firm; she earned $2.45 a hour. She found a new job in 1979 as a cutter in a necktie manufacturer where she cut lining for neckties. Her rate of pay increased to $3.30 an hour. Not until two years later, however, when her wages increased to $4.19 an hour could she leave welfare and support her three children on her own earnings. Alice's early decision to quit school but enter the labor market initiated the slow process of working off welfare, hampered by a lack of education and marketable job skills.

Working Off Welfare

A final issue is how women work their way off welfare when a new job does not result in an exit. The evidence presented thus far has shown that women who combine work and welfare are more disadvantaged in family resources and human capital than women who experience the more rapid job exits; therefore, they spend a longer time on welfare before working and while they work. Does their time in the workforce help them leave welfare eventually? To address this question, a final event history analysis of the transition off welfare among women who combine work and welfare is presented in table 7.4.

The results are again presented as the percentage change in the probability of welfare exit. Because the teenage mothers who combine work and welfare are selectively disadvantaged, they do not display any marked variation in their background characteristics. The background characteristics have the expected effects, but none are statistically significant. Changing life circumstances predominantly determine the route off welfare for working welfare mothers. Women work their way off welfare when they finish their high school education or through cumulative work experience. Working welfare mothers who attain a high school diploma increase their chances of welfare exit by 75 percent, compared to welfare mothers who do not finish high school. Each additional year of labor market activity improves the likelihood of working off welfare by 8 percent, as illustrated by Alice's experience. Further evidence of child care constraints prolonging welfare dependency is also

Table 7.4 Determinants of Welfare Exit among Women Who Combine Work and Welfare

Variable	% Change in Probability of Welfare Exit
< 16 at first pregnancy	−28
High educational aspirations	+17
At grade level	+36
At spell beginning:	
married	+52
3 or more children	−8
Cumulative work experience	+8*
Graduate high school	+75*
Preschool children present	−43*
Marry or cohabit	+125*
OBRA	−8
Rise in unemployment	−10

*Significant at the .05 level.

Note: See table B.14 for full set of parameter estimates and standard errors.

found. Women with preschool children to care for face a 43 percent lower odds of leaving welfare while working than working mothers with older children.

An alternative route off welfare for working mothers is through marriage or cohabitation. When mothers marry or enter a cohabiting relationship, their chances of welfare exit increase by 125 percent. For some women, their work effort is simply not enough to enable them to leave welfare, and only by obtaining an additional source of income through a partner can they exit welfare. Women who work part-time or at low-wage jobs cannot support their families on their labor market earnings. The structural effects of the OBRA legislation and unemployment conditions have less of an impact on the probability that the mother's work will move her off welfare than the factors that directly impact her work, such as child care constraints, increasing education and experience, and alternative sources of income.

Summary

Labor force participation by the welfare mothers in the Baltimore Study was surprisingly widespread throughout the study period. As a result, work provided the dominant route out of welfare dependency for teenage mothers. Women leave welfare through work in two ways: they either find a job that moves them off welfare, or they combine work and welfare until they eventually work their way off welfare through cumulative work experience. Welfare mothers who stay in school and finish their high school education secure a stable job and exit welfare rapidly. Women with fewer family and educational resources who do not experience the rapid job exits usually manage to find a job to supplement their welfare income. When these mothers eventually graduate from high school or build a substantial attachment to the workforce, they leave dependency and rely on job income alone. Women are especially able to leave welfare on their own earnings when they no longer need to care for preschool children.

Education is a crucial factor affecting labor force participation among welfare mothers. Women with more education have more human capital to invest in employment; hence, they are more likely to maintain a continuous attachment to the labor force (Moen 1985). For high-risk teenage mothers, graduating high school is their ticket out of welfare dependency through a high-paying job or a promotion and increase in earnings. Without a high school degree, mothers can only find unstable, low-wage jobs that provide little chance for advancement or further job training, requiring them to remain dependent on welfare (Harris 1993; Spalter-Roth and Hartmann 1994a).

The trade-off between work experience and education that young mothers face early in their welfare careers represents a critical choice that has a significant impact on subsequent welfare use. Mothers who follow the education path leave welfare quickly through a job and are less likely to return. Mothers who cut their education short and prematurely enter the workforce spend a much longer time working their way off welfare. Women who enter the labor force lacking job skills or training struggle to support their families at low-paying jobs with little opportunity for advancement.

These findings have important implications for welfare reform measures that aim to get welfare mothers into the labor force. Simply placing welfare mothers in jobs may not do much to improve their economic security or reduce state welfare costs. Without job skills and especially education, work does not equate with self-sufficiency. Furthermore, the underlying assumption that welfare mothers do not work nor want to work undermines the potential for welfare reform to reduce long-term dependency. This study has shown that even though welfare mothers are working, the welfare burden to families and society continues. The policy attention on nonwork is misplaced and misses the crucial issues. Policymakers should *not* be asking why recipients do not work, but rather they should ask why the work that welfare recipients *do* does not lift their families out of welfare.

This research suggests that among the Baltimore mothers, at least, welfare recipients worked out of economic need to support their families. In addition, the substantial amount of work activity displayed by the welfare mothers in Baltimore demonstrates that they were quite motivated to do so. However, work did not necessarily lift women out of dependency, at least initially, or insure a permanent exit, because welfare mothers predominately hold low-wage jobs without fringe benefits. Recipients who move into these jobs generally remain in poverty and must continue to combine income from work and welfare to provide for their families.

Chapter 8
Implications for Welfare Policy

This study has traced the welfare dynamics of a cohort of urban black women who experienced an adolescent birth when all of the teenagers were still in high school and most were unmarried. The adolescent childbearers were followed for a period of twenty years after their first birth, permitting me to track their subsequent life course trajectories that included work, marriage, cohabitation, subsequent childbearing, schooling, and living arrangements, and the way in which unfolding events along these trajectories intersected with their welfare trajectory. The research has focused on the processes of entering and exiting welfare dependency by explaining the determinants of welfare transitions. Individual characteristics, important life decisions, and life events that occurred to the young mother throughout her parental life course have a dynamic impact on welfare transitions and length of receipt. These same factors describe the different welfare careers of the adolescent childbearers in the Baltimore data.

Research Findings

Of the 288 adolescent childbearers who became parents at age eighteen or younger, two-thirds eventually depended on welfare at some point during the twenty years following the first birth. Although welfare touched the majority of women's lives, the average length of receipt was relatively short and chronic dependence on welfare was rare. About half of all initial spells of welfare were over within two years of receipt, but a third of the women experienced multiple spells of welfare. However, repeat spells ended more rapidly than initial spells. Only 4.1 percent were chronically dependent on welfare throughout the entire study period, and all but one of these women spent time working in the labor force. In fact, as welfare use became more persistent, so did the propensity to supplement welfare income with earnings from a job.

Transitions into welfare dependency were described differently for initial and return spells because they occurred at different stages within the mother's parental life course and depicted a different set of life circumstances. Initial entry into welfare occurred soon after the first birth when most of the Baltimore mothers were still teenagers or in their early twenties. Nearly a third began to receive welfare the same year they became teenage parents. For many of the adolescents, this early dependence on welfare enabled them to finish high school.

Marital dissolution, however, was the most powerful determinant of initial entry into welfare. Other events that precipitated initial receipt following the study birth were job loss and returning to school; whereas marriage by the time of the first birth and living with parents helped teen mothers avoid welfare receipt. The adolescents who were younger at first pregnancy, who had low educational goals, and whose parents received welfare were particularly prone to rapid first entry into public assistance.

Returns to welfare were caused primarily by job instability and factors that make the balance women must manage between their family and provider responsibilities more difficult, such as child care constraints and female headship. There also is an indication that welfare exits that occur through marriage or cohabitation are less stable than other exit routes, often leading to welfare return.

Transitions out of welfare dependency occurred predominantly through a job, as more than 60 percent of all spells ended when the mother found work. Marriage or cohabitation was another important cause of welfare exit, although this route was not as efficient as the work route. As a result, factors that enhanced the labor market success of young mothers were the important determinants of welfare exits. The human capital effects of education and work experience increased the likelihood of welfare exit by making it more likely that the mother could obtain a high-quality job. These effects were also likely to increase the marriageability of the young mother, with the greater economic security that she could bring to a relationship. In contrast, the presence of preschool children and poor labor market conditions with increasing unemployment reduced the chances that mothers would exit the program, making it especially difficult for women to work.

The Baltimore mothers left welfare through work in two ways: either they found a job that moved them off welfare, or they combined work and welfare until they eventually worked their way off welfare through cumulative work experience. Welfare mothers who stayed in school and finished their high school education secured a stable job and exited welfare rapidly. Women with fewer family and educational resources who did not experience the rapid job exits usually managed to find a job to supplement their welfare income. When these mothers eventually graduated from high school or built a substantial attachment to the workforce, they left welfare dependency by increasing either their wages or the hours they worked. Women are especially able to leave welfare on their own earnings when they no longer need to care for preschool children.

Exits through work were much more prevalent than exits through relationship changes among the Baltimore mothers. While this result agrees with recent studies that have analyzed monthly data on welfare transitions (e.g., Gritz and MaCurdy 1991; Harris 1993; Spalter-Roth and Hartmann 1994a; Pavetti 1993), it differs from Bane and Ellwood's studies (1983, 1994; Ellwood 1986) analyzing annual data from the PSID. They find that a quarter of all welfare spells end through work compared to the 63 percent that I find in the Baltimore data.

The main explanation for this difference is the way in which a work exit is defined. This study and the recent research using monthly data must rely on work status at the time of welfare exit to define a work exit. Bane and Ellwood, however, have reports of income in the PSID and define a work exit according to an increase in the annual earnings of the female head. In addition to formal employment, work status reports may reflect unreported income or work in the informal sector that welfare mothers may be more reluctant to report in standard earnings or income histories. The qualitative research of Edin and Jencks (1992) illustrates that "off-the-books" jobs are the norm among welfare mothers in order to maintain their family's economic viability (also see Edin and Lein 1996). Thus, the use of work status to define work exits may more accurately reflect the extent to which work and income-generating activities are associated with welfare transitions.

Work status reports are also more likely to capture work behavior during welfare spells, shown in the prevalence of combining work and welfare among the Baltimore mothers. In census and caseload statistics, the proportion of welfare recipients who report labor market earnings is never higher than 15 percent before 1981 and averages 5 to 6 percent post-OBRA, when the work incentives were eliminated (Moffitt 1992; U.S. House of Representatives 1994, table 10–28, CD line 3238). Yet in any given year in the Baltimore Study, about 50 percent of the mothers who were receiving welfare reported that they were also working, and over time in a spell the proportion who ever work increases further. Census data are based on reports of simultaneous receipt of income from earnings and from welfare at a point in time. Caseload data represent recipients' reports of labor market income to their case worker. Again, when recipients are asked to report whether or not they worked as opposed to how much income they received and from what sources, we find a much higher degree of work activity among welfare recipients than expected based on previous data.

Findings about the effects of parental welfare status are worth emphasizing. Women whose parents received welfare are significantly more likely to ever enter welfare than women whose parents never received welfare. The greater likelihood of welfare entry suggests an intergenerational effect of welfare receipt. However, I argue that this effect may represent more of a mechanical mechanism in which the pregnant teenager is simply added to the welfare family's household grant. Support for this interpretation is found by the lack of an intergenerational effect of parental welfare status on the *length* of receipt. The speed at which women exit the welfare program is not affected by their parents' welfare status. Mothers whose parents received welfare are no more likely to remain on welfare long term than mothers whose parents did not receive welfare.

The fact that parental welfare status increases the likelihood of receipt but not the persistence of receipt supports a structural perspective of the causes of long-term welfare dependency. To the extent that welfare use is transmitted culturally across the generations, it may exist in the greater likelihood of welfare entry as a result of exposure, but it does not exist in a greater likelihood of long-term receipt. A relationship between parents' welfare receipt and daughters' length of receipt does not even exist at the bivariate level (see fig. 5.1). Moreover, parental welfare receipt does not differentiate the women who work while they are on welfare from those who do not work, providing no support for a cultural perspective that would argue growing up in a welfare family encourages nonwork as a parent. Rather, parental welfare receipt differentiates the mothers who find jobs that move them off welfare from the mothers who find jobs that are not sufficient to move them off welfare, implying a lower socioeconomic status is associated with parental welfare status.

Overall, results from this study lend more support for a structural perspective of the causes of welfare transitions than a cultural interpretation. While background characteristics are important in determining initial welfare entry, when the mothers are young and many are still living at home, the most important predictors of welfare transitions are those factors that place mothers in a social context, such as marriage, female headship, or living with others, or in a structural position along a life course trajectory with differential access to resources and information, such as in school, in a job, or in a relationship. In general, background characteristics are mediated by the more-urgent life events that impinge directly on the mother's access to income sources and social support, and cause her to constantly adjust her economic strategy to provide for her family as her economic and social circumstances change.

Finally, the work and welfare behavior of teenage mothers is more similar to that for all single mothers found in previous studies than it is different. This finding is not that surprising given that many single mothers on welfare began childbearing as teenagers, but the presumption that teenage motherhood is synonymous with long-term receipt of public assistance is no more true than it is for single mothers in general. There are some minor differences, however. A larger proportion of teen mothers ever resort to welfare than single mothers in general, but their patterns of receipt are similar. About 50 percent of spells end within two years, more than a third return for repeat dependency, and a minority experience long-term receipt. Teen mothers experience slightly more persistence on welfare than all single mothers (see table 3.2), but this is not due to less work effort, as similar proportions work while on welfare and exit welfare through work (see Harris 1993). Because work is the main route by which all single mothers and former teenage mothers exit welfare, factors that inhibit work extend welfare receipt. Barriers to work are more severe for young mothers and probably explain their slightly longer cumulative receipt. This research consistently identified child care constraints and human capital deficiencies as factors that impede economic independence and as such, represent barriers to stable and secure jobs that probably loom larger among teen mothers than single mothers in general.

Types of Welfare Recipients

The welfare behavior of the Baltimore mothers described three types of welfare recipients: early-exit women, persistent recipients, and recidivists. Early-exit recipients had more favorable family and individual resources. They were among the oldest adolescents at first pregnancy, which gave them an educational advantage. As a result, early-exit women were more likely to graduate high school, successfully limit additional fertility, and enter more stable marriages. Many early-exit recipients began welfare receipt when the study child was born so that they could finish their education and secure a steady job—leaving welfare permanently after one or two years. Others depended briefly on welfare following job loss or an additional birth. With education and job skills, they quickly returned to work, found another job, or less frequently, married and never returned to welfare again.

In contrast, persistent recipients came from disadvantaged families with fewer social supports and family resources. They were the youngest at first pregnancy and were likely to drop out of high school, experience high additional fertility, and spend less time in the workforce and more time as a female head than other recipients. They entered welfare dependency early, at the time of or soon after the study birth. Lacking in educational resources, persistent recipients experienced long-term receipt, eventually exiting welfare through the slow process of combining work and welfare, or when they left female headship through marriage.

Cycling recipients displayed a revolving-door pattern of welfare use, which seemed to be a consequence of parallel erratic and changing life events. The favorable family influences of a two-parent household during adolescence and a working mother as a role model is reflected in the cyclers' determination to leave welfare dependency. However, lacking in educational and job skills, and burdened by a larger number of children than the other recipients, the cyclers were continually vulnerable to events that threatened their attempts at self-sufficiency, particularly marital and job instability.

Early Marriage

One of the most consistent findings in this research is the implication that early marriage often leads to either persistent or episodic spells of welfare receipt given the rather high dissolution rates of early marriage among the Baltimore mothers (Furstenberg, Brooks-Gunn, and Morgan 1987). The revolving-door welfare behavior of the cycler, in particular, can often be traced back to the early life decision to marry at the time of or soon after the birth of the first child.

Cyclers were shown to enter marriage early and were overrepresented among the adolescents who married before the birth of the study child. They were also found to discontinue their educational activity early in the study period, probably when they entered marriage. They were least likely to use birth control and thus experienced the most rapid subsequent fertility. And, unfortunately, they experienced the most marital instability, as 40 percent of the women who married before or shortly after the study birth had an early divorce and only one in three of these early marriages were intact seventeen years later (Furstenberg, Brooks-Gunn, and Morgan 1987).

JoAnn, the case history of a cycling recipient, illustrates this pattern. JoAnn was seventeen, unmarried, and in the eleventh grade when she was pregnant. She married the father of her child six months after her son was born. Her husband was also seventeen and had dropped out of school in the eighth grade. He worked as a laborer, but his income was still low enough so that they qualified for welfare. After JoAnn got married, she dropped out of school and had another child by the time she was nineteen. During the third interview, JoAnn expressed regret over her early decision to marry. She explained that she would have preferred to marry later and only married for the sake of the baby. She stated that she was much happier four or five years ago "because I really didn't want to get married and I did because of [son]." When asked if there was one thing she would change if she could as she thought back over the past few years, she answered, "my marriage." Her marriage lasted three years.

Marital breakup was related to longer periods of welfare receipt compared to other beginning types. Moreover, marital dissolution early in the parental life course, when the mothers were still teenagers or in their early twenties, caused greater persistence on welfare than later in the life course. The earlier the marriage, the more likely the young mother abandoned her education and experienced additional fertility. When the marriage dissolved, the woman entered female headship and welfare dependency without educational resources and with many children to support.

Although the cycling women were quite motivated to get off welfare, exhibited by their repeated attempts, with the additional burdens of a large family and deficiencies in education, their efforts were often thwarted. Moreover, the instability in the cycler's young family life carried over to her working career, which experienced substantial job instability, causing the female head to move in and out of welfare dependency like a revolving door, alternating between work and welfare.

There is some indication that this same process occurred to young mothers who left initial welfare dependency through marriage or cohabitation, since relationship exits were found to be the least permanent. Subsequent fertility and the curtailment of education associated with marriage again put the young mother at greater risk of longer cumulative receipt through multiple spells of welfare or a sporadic work history if the young relationship failed. The volatility of early marriage had a significant impact on the young mothers' subsequent economic circumstances.

Timing of Events

The early adolescent birth caused young women to enter the role of parenthood "off schedule" and set in motion an acceleration of other roles or life trajectories (Elder 1985). The events of high school graduation, marriage, and additional fertility interact in a dynamic way and have varying impacts on subsequent welfare dependency according to when these events occurred within the young mother's parental life course. A cycling pattern of welfare receipt, for example, was largely explained by life events that occurred soon after the study birth. Early marriage, nonuse of birth control, the curtailment of education, and early welfare entry led to a revolving-door pattern of welfare dependence associated with sporadic work experience and female headship.

The onset of female headship at the time of the first teenage birth for unmarried adolescents caused less persistence on welfare than the onset of female headship due to marital dissolution. At the time of the first birth, adolescents who entered welfare had only one child and most were still in school. With marriage, family sizes grow, and many teen mothers leave school for good.

This research also revealed that the effects of job loss and marital breakup differentially affect welfare transitions depending on when they occur. Soon after the birth of the study child, the mother is more vulnerable to marriage or cohabitation breakup and less sensitive to job loss than she is later in her life course after already experiencing female headship and having more of an investment in working. Thus, changes in family structure influenced welfare transitions early in the study period when the mother had little work experience and young children, while employment factors determined welfare transitions later in the study period.

Young mothers face a number of trade-offs early in their life course as parents, and the choices they make about marriage, education, and work have lasting effects on their subsequent well-being. Trade-offs between family activities involving marriage and subsequent childbearing, and human capital activities involving schooling or work play a significant role in the kinds of economic strategies mothers can employ if the family route is shaken by marital dissolution. The trade-off between work experience and education that young mothers face early in their welfare spells represents a critical choice that has a significant impact on subsequent welfare use. Mothers who follow the education path leave welfare quickly through a job and are less likely to return. Mothers who cut their education short and prematurely enter the workforce spend a much longer time working their way off welfare.

These difficult trade-offs and differential impacts of early life course decisions are exemplified in the contrasts among the three case studies of types of welfare recipients. Chandra chose the education route early on, which enabled her to rely on welfare briefly and exit to a decent job. Chandra eventually married and continued to work. She did have three additional children, but Chandra remained stably married and never returned to welfare. Alice chose the work route early on, but was severely disadvantaged by her young age and lack of work experience and education. Alice remained on welfare for fifteen years, working nearly the entire time, until she finally worked her way off in the early 1980s. Alice never finished school, never married, and had two additional children outside of marriage, though she did maintain a long-term cohabitation for fourteen years. JoAnn chose the family route, marrying to legitimate her birth and having a quick subsequent birth. She dropped out of school and was slow to enter the workforce. After her first marriage broke up, after a spell of six years on welfare, and after exiting through a new co-habitation, JoAnn entered the labor market. This contact with the work-force helped her exit her second spell of welfare when her second marriage ended.

Policy Considerations

A question remains that cannot be directly addressed with these data: Are women better off when they leave welfare? Undoubtedly, early-exit women are, but they used welfare for temporary assistance while they finished their schooling or searched for a job. Their transitions off welfare were supported by education and less hampered by a large family, and they had higher earning abilities and enjoyed greater employment opportunities.

But does the motivation and determination of cyclers to repeatedly leave welfare dependency translate into eventual economic security and stable employment? Are they better off than persistent recipients who have longer stays on welfare until they find work or marry? The cyclers' motivation to achieve independence from welfare is admirable, and they may appear to impose a smaller societal cost than persistent recipients in terms of welfare expenditures. However, there is evidence that the in-stability they experienced in their marital and employment careers bears a high individual cost.

Table 8.1 displays the family income levels reported at time 5, at the seventeen-year follow-up, by type of recipient. The differences are rather dramatic. More than 70 percent of the cyclers have family incomes of less than ten thousand dollars, below the poverty line for a family of four in 1984. About half the persistent recipients are living in poverty,

Table 8.1 Percent Distribution of Family Income by Type of Recipient, Time 5 (1984)

Family Income	Recipient Type			
	Never used Welfare	Early Exit	Persistent	Cycler
<$10,000	5.1	17.9	50.6	71.2
$10,000–$24,999	46.8	53.6	31.6	22.7
$25,000+	48.1	28.6	17.7	6.1
Total	100%	100%	100%	100%

and only 18 percent of early-exit women are in the lowest income range. Of course, the women who never received welfare during the study enjoy the highest levels of socioeconomic status as almost half have family incomes above twenty-five thousand dollars, compared to nearly 30 percent of the early-exit women and 18 percent of the persistent recipients. Cyclers are much less likely to fare so well, with only 6 percent in the highest income range in 1984. Family income is only one measure of economic well-being and is highly related to marital status. Nevertheless, this distribution suggests that the stability of remaining on welfare for longer periods, possibly supplementing this income with a job and slowly attaining more education, may be better in the long run than struggling at economic independence when one is so vulnerable to repeated setbacks and job instability.

The quantitative pattern is consistent with the qualitative data on the three types of recipients. By the end of the study, twenty years after the first teenage birth, Chandra is faring the best. Although her fourth child is only three years old, Chandra works as a bookkeeper at a furniture store making $7.00 an hour. Her husband works as a driver for a private company that makes deliveries. Together they have a savings account, a checking account, and credit cards. Alice, who relied on welfare for fifteen years, was working as a housekeeper in 1987. She cleaned clinics in a university medical center, making $6.81 an hour. Her job provided paid sick leave, medical benefits, and paid vacations. Alice was the sole adult in a household that included three children and one grandchild. She did not have a checking account or a credit card, nor did she own a car or have a driver's license, but she did have a savings account. JoAnn, the cycling recipient, was the worse off twenty years after the first teenage birth. JoAnn was also the sole adult in the household, living with her two adolescent sons, aged seventeen and nineteen. She worked as a cashier and waitress at a food service at $5.00 an hour. Her job also provided paid sick leave, medical benefits, and paid vacation, benefits which are probably instrumental in her ability to remain off welfare at such a low wage rate. At the age of thirty-six, with two teenage sons, JoAnn does not have a checking account, a savings account, a credit card, a car, or a driver's license.

Policymakers are most concerned with chronic welfare dependence and the small number of recipients who account for the bulk of the welfare budget. This is a valid policy issue as the selection process of exiting welfare leaves behind the most disadvantaged women with low levels of education, resources, and employment probabilities. However, this research has shown that persistent dependency, defined as more than two years on welfare, often helped young mothers to eventually graduate high school, obtain work experience, and ultimately achieve some measure of self-reliance.

Cyclers, on the other hand, are motivated to leave welfare and exit quickly and repeatedly. But perhaps in doing so, they do not have the chance to invest in the accumulation of additional resources and thus end up worse off in terms of job stability and income. Even though the persistent recipients obtain less education than the cycling recipients overall, they do not return to welfare once they leave, while the cycling recipients exit sooner, on average, but return for multiple spells. It is possible that the more-persistent recipients are able to maintain their welfare exits because they took more time on welfare to get their lives back on track and devise a way to exit welfare permanently, while the cycling recipients may have exited before they were able to sustain their exits. Women who are unprepared for the harsh realities of minimum-wage jobs, turnover in child care arrangements, or the marital strains of living in poverty may find themselves cycling back onto welfare often.

While the women with more education, fewer children, and recent work experience are more likely to exit welfare quickly and remain off welfare, the women without those advantages must struggle with fewer resources to come up with a strategy for remaining off welfare. Persistent and cycling recipients are more disadvantaged than early-exit women, and their different welfare behaviors have different consequences. Persistent women rely on welfare for longer periods, remaining poor and disadvantaged. But they do not seem to experience the tremendous marital and job instability of cycling women, which repeatedly puts them at risk for subsequent welfare receipt and seems to have long-term consequences as well.

Too much of the policy focus has been on chronic welfare dependence and not enough attention has been paid to cycling patterns of welfare. Short-sighted policy goals of moving women off welfare may consider welfare exiting a sign of success, missing the core of welfare dynamics and welfare dependence. Other recent studies have also shown the prevalence of cycling welfare behavior (Bane and Ellwood 1994; Ellwood 1986), and studies that examine monthly data report even higher rates of welfare return than studies based on annual data (see Harris 1993; Pavetti 1993; Spalter-Roth and Hartmann 1994a). From an individual and a societal point of view, exits are only a success if women can remain off welfare. Evidence suggests that the economic security following welfare exit is precarious and that usually former welfare mothers cannot sustain their exits on one source of income because that source is commonly too low or too unstable among poor mothers (Bane and Ellwood 1994; Edin and Lein 1996; Harris 1996; Spalter-Roth, Hartmann, and Andrews 1993). The heart of the issue, therefore, is not whether women exit welfare, but whether former welfare mothers can stay off welfare. Only when welfare policies focus on this type of welfare behavior will they attain some success in reducing welfare dependency.

Work Policies

How can policies sustain and reinforce welfare exits? The place to start is to first recognize the considerable work effort that is demonstrated by women on welfare, even by teenage mothers thought to eschew the value of a work ethic. This study has documented substantial labor market activity among teenage mothers on welfare not expected by the previous research on teenage childbearing or by the public's disconcerting view of early nonmarital childbearing. On average, half the women receiving welfare during each year of the study were supplementing welfare income with their own earnings from a job. Exclusive dependence on welfare occurred primarily in the beginning of the study period when the mothers were still in school and had very little job experience or earning ability. The dominant routes off welfare were through work, as more than 60 percent of all spells ended when the mother was actively employed.

Despite the importance of these findings, work is not the solution it appears to be. In fact, the persistent and cycling recipients in the Baltimore Study would probably argue that work is the problem rather than the solution. The extensive work demonstrated by the teen mothers on welfare was often not enough to help them leave welfare and often not enough to help them maintain their welfare exits. Although a job was the most efficient route out of dependency for women experiencing a premarital birth in adolescence, without the educational skills or previous work experience to maintain employment, return dependency was likely.

Thus, welfare policy that simply places recipients in a job will not succeed in securing long-term independence from welfare. Lawmakers need to focus on how policies can support the work that welfare mothers do so that they can maintain their families in decency and still balance their provider role with their parenting role.

The foundation of employment and training on which welfare reform is currently based is well advised and well intended. Evaluations of experimental state welfare-to-work programs implemented in the 1980s have generally concluded that training and job search assistance produced gains in employment and total earnings among female AFDC recipients (Friedlander and Burtless 1995; Gueron and Pauly 1991). The programs were also found to be cost effective in that the gains in participants' earnings and the reduction in AFDC payments more than offset program costs. However, the earnings gains were small and were achieved through increases in work hours, not wage rates, which has historically been the consequence of work programs in a disadvantaged population (Bassi 1984; Bassi and Ashenfelter 1986; Blank 1994; Levy 1982). Program participants did not obtain better-paying jobs nor did they find jobs with better job security, and the recipients who secured long-term employment did so at very low wages (Friedlander and Burtless 1995). Because earnings gains were offset with reductions in AFDC benefits, the total family incomes of program participants as workers were hardly different from their total incomes as welfare recipients, both below the poverty line.

Welfare-to-work programs that have more extensive support services to promote education and job training show better results, but cost more (see Maynard 1993). Given the current state of the economy and government budget concerns in the 1990s, heavy investment in jobs programs for welfare recipients is not likely to reach state or federal agendas. At some point in the welfare reform discussions, we have to recognize the limits of education and training programs. While the programs may help recipients find jobs, they are unlikely to increase recipients' human capital appreciably or enhance their marketable skills measurably, factors that would allow women to command a wage rate in today's economy that can provide for families on their earnings alone. Women may find jobs, and they may work for some time at the minimum wage, but without avenues for job advancement or wage growth, and sometimes without medical benefits, juggling the demands of caring for children, arranging child care and transportation, and sacrificing time with children may not seem worth it. If we want to reduce welfare dependency without increasing human suffering, the challenge for policy is to make this work worth it.

This research shows that teenage mothers who end up on welfare want to work and do work, but they face numerous barriers to maintaining stable employment and to sufficiently providing for their families. Why not support the work that welfare mothers do with supplemental income that rewards work and with support services to help young mothers balance their parenting roles with their provider roles? Policies that include provisions for job and education training, child care, and health care will remove some of the barriers welfare mothers face as they work their way off welfare and enhance the stability of their employment.

Education and training are important aspects of any work program designed to move welfare mothers into the labor force, but given their likely funding restraints, it will be difficult for recipients to land a high-quality job in the transition off welfare. There are two essential components, however, that would reinforce this transition and support the work of poor mothers: health insurance and child care. Currently the welfare program provides health insurance to recipients and their children through the medicaid program, and women on welfare who also work are provided child care. These benefits are lost when mothers move off welfare. It is extremely difficult for families with access to only low-wage jobs to survive off welfare unless these two essential needs are met. Moreover, what many would consider a responsible mother would not put her children at risk without access to health care. If women did receive medical insurance and child care provisions, then a mother could provide for herself and two children in a full-time job at the minimum wage if she received supplements from the Earned Income Tax Credit, which rewards her work, and food stamp programs that already are available.

Even the Baltimore mothers with very young children were working in the labor market to maintain their families. Rather than exempt AFDC mothers with young children (under three) from the work program, let them have the choice to participate and have access to the services so that their work efforts can be supported by such measures as well. One reason the Baltimore mothers could not provide for their families on their own earnings was the presence of many or young children, as child care constraints are greater for young mothers. Provisions for child care will enable mothers to find work or permit those who work part-time to enter full-time positions, possibly obtain additional benefits, and leave welfare.

A third aspect that would support working poor mothers is housing assistance. Qualitative work shows that food and rent expenses subsume nearly all of the median total of welfare benefits and food stamps, and similarly, nearly all the monthly pay of low-wage work (Edin and Lein 1996). Moreover, most poor women pay market rent for their housing. More housing assistance, especially to women in high-rent areas, would help working mothers exit and stay off of welfare.

The idea that welfare recipients need work requirements in order to get them into the labor market is out of touch with the realities of welfare mothers' lives. Policymakers need to pay attention to the conditions of work among welfare mothers not on the presence or absence of work effort. If the current work by welfare mothers is supported by guaranteeing health insurance, providing child care, and offering more housing assistance, in addition to the earned income tax credit and food stamps supplements that already exist in our social welfare program, women could support their families on the earnings they receive from work. This study repeatedly showed that more than one source of income was necessary to move women off welfare and to sustain their exits. Welfare reform and work programs that provide these additional sources of income in the form of health care, child care, and housing benefits, will do more to reduce welfare dependency in U.S. society than imposing work requirements on women who are already working or want to work.

In addition to increased work obligations from welfare recipients, future welfare policies will likely impose time limits on lifetime receipt. Many states have already set their own time limits with the goal of moving recipients more quickly into jobs with the knowledge that they can not fall back on welfare if their jobs do not work out. The purpose of time-limited receipt is to insure that long-term dependence on welfare does not occur and to require the welfare poor to work, regardless of the family context or the work conditions—including the adequacy of wages, work hours, and provisions for health care or child care. These measures will largely affect persistent and cycling recipients portrayed by the mothers in the Baltimore Study. Based on what we have learned about these two types of recipients, the impact of time-limited welfare could be rather detrimental for the persistent women, especially without support services for low-wage work.

Recall that the persistent women were those who had one spell of welfare that lasted for more than two years, the welfare time limit recently chosen in the state of North Carolina. Although a few of the persistent women have chronic receipt, most receive welfare anywhere from three to eight years. The persistent women, however, were the most disadvantaged with respect to their earning abilities and needed a longer time to develop a strategy for leaving welfare. Time limits will force these women into low-wage work earlier, making them look like the cyclers, but with fewer resources and skills for paid work. The consequences will probably resemble the life course of the cycling women, where sudden events trigger change and instability in other life course trajectories, including not only work but also living arrangements, schooling, and other relationships. Although persistent women spent longer on welfare than the other recipients, in the long run they fared better than the cyclers, whose long-term economic situation reflected the toll of repeated setbacks and instability. Therefore, time limits will probably extend this insecurity for cycling recipients and create more instability in the lives of persistent recipients. Provisions of support services for work may help, but the main casualties of instability in the context of poverty will be children.

The purpose of the AFDC program is to provide economic support for the care of dependent children, yet the well-being of children is rarely mentioned in discussions of welfare reform. We have seen that women who move from welfare to work through job programs seldom improve the economic situation of their families, but there may be other benefits for the mother, such as expanded social networks in the world of work and an increased sense of self-worth and accomplishment. However, whether children benefit when welfare mothers work is unknown. Their economic circumstances remain relatively the same, but their home environment will change with the loss of mother's time and supervision, and with possible exposure to substitute care. We have yet to understand the consequences of these changes for the well-being of poor children, but future welfare policies in the form of intensified work requirements and time-limited receipt is sure to bring on these changes.

Appendix A
Reliability of Data

A measure of reliability indicates the level of consistency between two responses to a similar question at different points in time. When Furstenberg analyzed the reliability of the marriage and school data, he found estimates of Cronbach's alpha to average .77 (see appendix B in Furstenberg, Brooks-Gunn, and Morgan 1987, 158–60). Information from the life history calendar was compared with reports on marital status and level of schooling at all four interviews in the first phase of the study by matching the interview years with the same years on the calendar. The authors consider this level of reliability to be relatively high since an alpha of .60 is considered acceptable for sound data analysis.

Furstenberg further notes that inconsistencies may be explained by the fact that questions regarding the same event from the two points in time were nonparallel in reference to the timing of the response. The interview questions ask women their marital status while the calendar translates a marriage history into years of marriage. If a woman was single in the beginning of the year when she was interviewed but married later in the same year, she would be recorded as unmarried in the interview but married on the calendar (since the observation unit is a year). Similarly, the school year and calendar year cover different months and thus the interview reporting of completion of school may be inconsistent with the calendar information.

The reliability of the welfare data was analyzed by Furstenberg and his colleagues (1987) only at the five-year follow-up (time 4) because welfare questions in previous interviews were nonparallel to the respective point of reference in the calendar. An alpha of .70 was estimated for the reliability of the welfare responses at the five-year follow-up. Furstenberg states that "respondents are more likely to 'forget' having been on welfare than to 'admit' receipt of welfare which originally they denied" (Furstenberg et al., 1987, p.160).

The extent to which reports of welfare use at the same point in time

145

are consistent is examined below, keeping in mind the nonparallel nature of these reports. For example, in the early interviews, the women only reported current welfare status at the time of the interview, which may have varied throughout the calendar year; while the calendar recorded welfare use over the entire year. However, for the sake of comparison, the distribution of consistency in responses between the time 2, time 3, and time 4 interview questions and the retrospective reporting of welfare receipt on the life history calendar is shown in table A.1.

The level of consistency in correctly recalling welfare receipt during the earlier interview year is reassuringly constant, increasing slightly with time. However, the degree to which women "forget" receipt of welfare increases with time. Mentioned previously, the calendar reporting of welfare use is likely to miss short spells of receipt that may last for a few months within the year. Since only current welfare status was recorded at the time 2 and time 3 interviews, these measures also miss short spells of welfare that occur at other points during the interview year. Therefore, some of the underreporting cancels out. The higher level of underreporting at the time 4 interview may occur because the time 4 interview inquired about welfare receipt throughout the year and was more likely to capture short durations of welfare, whereas the calendar recording of welfare use during the time 4 interview year may have missed the relatively short spells of receipt due to recall error of the respondent.

Because this research focuses on transitions into and out of welfare dependency and not on the precise amount of time spent on welfare, the information regarding the transitions that I observe should be fairly accurate and relate to other changing life course events that are also observed on a yearly basis. Moreover, the consistency of correct responses to welfare questions over time suggests that the patterns of movement in and out of welfare are reliably reflected in the data throughout the study period. Overall, the reliability measures of the Baltimore data examined by Furstenberg and his colleagues (1987) are quite acceptable.

Table A.1 The Consistency of Reporting Welfare Receipt (Percentages)

Calendar Report	Time 2	Time 3	Time 4
Consistent Response	75.1	76.3	78.5
Underreported Welfare Receipt	8.3	10.2	15.4
N	181	266	247

Appendix B
Methods of Analysis

Life table techniques are us to describe the length of welfare receipt and subsequent nonreceipt and the patterns of returning to welfare (Namboodiri and Suchindran 1987). Event history methods are then applied to analyze the transitions into and out of welfare receipt (Allison 1982, 1984; Tuma and Hannan 1984; Yamaguchi 1991). A discrete-time model is used because welfare status is not measured exactly, but rather in discrete annual units. The dependent variable is a transition either into or out of welfare, indicated by a change in welfare status from one year to the following consecutive year.

An advantage of survival techniques, used in life table methods and event history methods, is that the information from right-censored observations is not wasted but rather is included in the analysis. Right censoring occurs when the study period ends before a woman is observed to experience the particular event of interest (i.e., the twenty-year follow-up interview occurs before a woman exits a spell of welfare). By including information on her spell duration and the fact that she did not experience the event of interest, unbiased and more reliable estimates of the probability of event occurrence in a dynamic framework are obtained.

Explanatory variables include both fixed and time-varying variables. Time-invariant factors include family background variables and individual characteristics; time-varying covariates change annually. The list of fixed and time-varying covariates used throughout analyses is shown in table B.1.

In a discrete-time model, the dependent variable is the probability that a welfare transition will occur at a particular duration for those at risk to the transition of interest. To illustrate with the welfare exit model, the dependent variable is the probability that a transition from welfare receipt

147

at time t to no receipt at time t+1 will occur for all those on welfare at time t. Time, or duration, is measured in years, where year 1 is the first year of receipt in a spell of welfare. To explain the process of exiting welfare, the exit probability, denoted as P_t, is estimated as a function of the explanatory variables using a logit transformation. Using maximum likelihood methods, the basic model estimated is:

$$\log \frac{P_{it}}{1-P_{it}} = \alpha + \beta X_i + \Phi Z_{it}$$

where P_{it} = probability of welfare exit for individual i at time t;
$\quad\quad\;\; X$ = vector of time-invariant independent variables; and
$\quad\quad\;\; Z_t$ = vector of time-varying independent variables at each time, t.

As P_t varies between 0 and 1, the left-hand side of the equation, the logit, varies between minus and plus infinity for $t = 1, \ldots 22$.[1] The X variables vary across individuals but are constant over time and thus measure between-subject variation (e.g., parental receipt of welfare, age at pregnancy). The Z variables measure between- and within-subject variation, as values on each specific variable can vary over time for an individual (e.g., education, work status, family size). The coefficients, β and Φ, estimate the effects of differences across individuals and changes in variable levels or states between and within individuals across time.

Duration is specified in the model by allowing a different base (or intercept) exit probability during the first two years of a spell of welfare receipt, and for durations of receipt lasting three years or more. This specifies that the rate of welfare exit differs in the first and second year of a spell of welfare, but beyond two years of receipt, the rate of exit does not vary with time. This specification of time dependence is based on exploratory analysis (not shown) of the baseline hazard function of welfare exit by duration in a spell and is similar to a piecewise exponential hazard model in continuous-time models, which assumes that the baseline hazard rate is constant within specified intervals of time (Yamaguchi 1991). Exploratory analysis also indicated that the hazard function of leaving welfare differed depending on whether a woman was in her first spell of welfare or in a return spell (see figure 3.1). Therefore, the exit models include a control variable for spell number in analyses that pool all welfare spells.

Although I have used the exit transition to illustrate the specifications of the event history model, the equation above applies to the general transition model used to analyze all welfare transitions in this research. Welfare entry transitions are modeled separately for the initial entry following the first teenage birth, and return entry following a previous exit from welfare. In the initial entry model, women are at risk to welfare entry at the time of the first teenage birth. Therefore, duration, or time, is measured in years from the first birth, and women can enter welfare at time 0, or in the same year as the first birth. Women at risk to reentry are all those women who ever enter a spell of welfare and exit, and time is measured in years since welfare exit. Duration is similarly specified in the entry models by allowing a different base entry probability during the years or interval of years in which the hazard rate changes over time following first birth or welfare exit.

An extension of the general equation is used in chapter 7 when I classify the dependent variable to define specific types of transitions. In particular, I examine the transition to work among mothers on welfare by whether the work transition results in welfare exit. The dependent variable is therefore a trichotomy: work transition and welfare exit, work transition and no welfare exit, and no work transition. While I use the same approach to the model specification, the estimation procedures differ slightly.[2] When the dependent variable is a dichotomy, I estimate a logistic regression model using maximum likelihood methods. In chapter 7 when the dependent variable is polytomous, I use maximum likelihood procedures to estimate a multinomial logistic regression.

The array of fixed and time-varying variables used throughout analyses in this book is described in table B.1. Among the time-varying measures, different operationalizations of activities or events in the same domain of a life trajectory may appear in the various models. For instance, in some models cumulative work experience measures activity in the work domain, while in other models work activity is measured by the events of finding a job or losing a job.

149

Appendix B: Methods of Analysis

Table B.1.   Description of Variables Used in Analysis

Family Background

Parental education:
    1 = the teen's mother or the father had at least a high school education.
    0 = both parents had less than a high school education.
Mother's family size:
    1 = 4 or more siblings.
    0 = 3 or fewer siblings.
Mother was a teen mother:
    1 = yes.
    0 = no.
Mother worked when daughter was an adolescent:
    1 = yes.
    0 = no.
Family structure in adolescence:
    1 = one-parent household.
    0 = two-parent household.
Parents' welfare receipt:
    1 = parents received welfare.
    0 = parents never received welfare.

Individual Characteristics

Age at first pregnancy:
    1 = less than 16 years old.
    0 = 16 years old or older.
Married at first birth:
    1 = yes.
    0 = no.
Educational aspirations:
    1 = high, post-secondary education.
    0 = low, high school or less.
At grade level:
    1 = yes, at appropriate grade for age.
    0 = no, failed at least one grade.
Attended special school for pregnant teens:
    1 = yes.
    0 = no.
Using birth control one year after first birth (T2):
    1 = yes.
    0 = no.

Life Events

If the event occurred in the year of observation, the variable is coded with a 1, otherwise its value is 0 in all years in which the event did not occur.

Additional birth
Marital dissolution (including separation or divorce)
Cohabitation breakup (partner and mother no longer live together)
Marriage
New cohabitation
Graduate high school this year
Lose job
Find a job

Table B.1. *(continued)*

Life Statuses

For each year that the mother occupies a particular status, the variable is coded with a 1, otherwise its value is 0 for the years in which the mother does not occupy the status.

Female headship (only adult in the household)
Living with mother
In school, before high school graduation
Graduated high school
Post-secondary education
Preschool children present in household
Has previous work experience

Cumulative Measures

Current age
Cumulative work experience (years worked)
Family size (number of children)
Cumulative years lived with mother

Contextual Variables

OBRA:
> 1 = year is 1981 or later, when OBRA legislation was in effect.
> 0 = year is pre-OBRA (i.e., before 1981).

Unemployment rate:
> actual rate for Baltimore metropolitan area in specific year (U.S. Department of Labor 1969, 1973, 1975, 1977, 1979, 1981, 1983, 1985, 1987, 1989).

Model Specification

Duration is measured with a set of dummy variables whose value is 1 when the mother is at that particular duration in a spell of welfare or nonwelfare (in entry models). For instance, year 1 would indicate that the mother is in the first year of the spell.

Spell number is controlled in the exit models in which first and return spells of welfare are pooled.

151

Table B.2   The Conditional Probability and Cumulative Proportion Exiting
Welfare by Length of Receipt in Initial and Return Spells

	Initial Spells of Receipt (N = 204)	
Duration (years)	**Conditional Probability**	**Cumulative Proportion**
1	0.32	0.32
2	0.25	0.49
3	0.13	0.56
4	0.07	0.59
5	0.10	0.62
6	0.07	0.65
7	0.07	0.68
8	0.06	0.70
9	0.10	0.73
10	0.09	0.75
11	0.04	0.76
12	0.09	0.79
13	0.19	0.83
14	0.10	0.84
15+	0.58	0.93
	Return Spells of Receipt (N = 91)	
Duration (years)	**Conditional Probability**	**Cumulative Proportion**
1	0.37	0.37
2	0.29	0.55
3	0.09	0.59
4	0.31	0.72
5	0.21	0.78
6	0.12	0.80
7	0.18	0.84
8+	0.40	0.90

Table B.3 The Conditional Probability and Cumulative Proportion Entering Welfare by Duration for Initial and Return Spells

Duration (years since first birth)	Initial Spells (N = 288)	
	Conditional Probability	**Cumulative Proportion**
1	0.29	0.29
2	0.11	0.37
3	0.08	0.42
4	0.07	0.46
5	0.04	0.48
6	0.09	0.52
7	0.07	0.56
8	0.05	0.58
9	0.04	0.60
10	0.06	0.62
11	0.05	0.64
12	0.06	0.66
13	0.03	0.67
14	0.01	0.67
15+	0.11	0.71

Duration (years since welfare exit)	Return Spells (N = 246)	
	Conditional Probability	**Cumulative Proportion**
1	0.08	0.08
2	0.07	0.15
3	0.08	0.22
4	0.06	0.26
5	0.01	0.27
6	0.04	0.30
7	0.02	0.32
8	0.05	0.35
9	0.03	0.37
10+	0.22	0.51

Table B.4 Cumulative Proportion Entering Initial Spell of Welfare by Family Background Characteristics

Years Since First Birth	Parents' Education		Mother a Teen Mother	
	< H.S.	≥ H.S.	Yes	No
1	0.30	0.33	0.32	0.28
2	0.39	0.39	0.40	0.36
3	0.46	0.40	0.46	0.41
4	0.49	0.46	0.49	0.47
5	0.52	0.48	0.52	0.49
6	0.56	0.52	0.55	0.54
7	0.60	0.52	0.58	0.58
8	0.60	0.58	0.60	0.60
9	0.63	0.58	0.61	0.63
10+	0.73	0.70	0.73	0.73
N	184	67	166	83

Years Since First Birth	Parents' Welfare Receipt**		Family Structure in Adolescence*	
	Yes	No	Single Parent	Two Parents
1	0.44	0.25	0.39	0.30
2	0.58	0.31	0.50	0.37
3	0.61	0.38	0.57	0.41
4	0.64	0.43	0.61	0.46
5	0.66	0.45	0.66	0.47
6	0.69	0.50	0.66	0.54
7	0.70	0.54	0.72	0.56
8	0.70	0.56	0.72	0.59
9	0.72	0.58	0.73	0.62
10+	0.83	0.70	0.83	0.74
N	64	194	82	142

*Differences significant at the .05 level.

**Differences significant at the .01 level.

Table B.5 Cumulative Proportion Entering Initial Spell of Welfare by Individual Characteristics at Time of Pregnancy

Years Since First Birth	Age at First Pregnancy**		Married at First Birth**	
	<16	16+	No	Yes
1	0.40	0.26	0.34	0.13
2	0.51	0.32	0.42	0.18
3	0.57	0.37	0.46	0.24
4	0.65	0.40	0.50	0.32
5	0.66	0.42	0.52	0.32
6	0.74	0.46	0.57	0.37
7	0.79	0.49	0.60	0.40
8	0.79	0.51	0.62	0.45
9	0.81	0.53	0.63	0.47
10+	0.87	0.66	0.74	0.58
N	68	220	226	62

Years Since First Birth	Educational Aspirations**		At Grade Level	
	Low	High	No	Yes
1	0.38	0.20	0.32	0.28
2	0.44	0.29	0.40	0.36
3	0.51	0.32	0.46	0.40
4	0.55	0.36	0.50	0.44
5	0.57	0.38	0.50	0.47
6	0.62	0.42	0.57	0.51
7	0.67	0.44	0.63	0.54
8	0.69	0.46	0.63	0.56
9	0.70	0.49	0.63	0.59
10+	0.80	0.61	0.79	0.68
N	150	138	72	216

* Differences significant at the .05 level.

** Differences significant at the .01 level.

Table B.6 Parameter Estimates of the Probability of Initial Welfare Entry

Explanatory Variables	1 b	1 SE	2 b	2 SE	3 b	3 SE
Duration:						
year 1	1.12	0.30	−2.00	0.35	−1.72	0.30
year 2	−.21	0.34	−1.61	0.37	−1.57	0.33
>2 years	—	—	—	—	—	—
Parental education ≥H.S.	−.01	0.22	−0.11	0.24		
Mother a teen mother	−.25	0.20	−0.24	0.22		
Two parent household	−.11	0.20	−0.11	0.23		
Parents receive welfare	−.75	0.22	0.71	0.24	0.44	0.19
<16 at first pregnancy	−.32	0.22	0.23	0.25		
High educational aspirations	−.85	0.20	−0.74	0.21	−0.68	0.17
At grade level	.05	0.22	0.06	0.24		
Married at first birth	−.18	0.33	−0.69	0.39	−0.75	0.24
Using birth control, T2	−.30	0.19	−0.12	0.21		
Age			−0.15	0.03	−0.17	0.02
In high school			1.31	0.28	1.46	0.24
Cumulative years with mother			−0.25	0.06	−0.15	0.05
Additional birth			0.13	0.27	0.11	0.22
Marital breakup			1.61	0.30	1.68	0.23
Cohabitation breakup			0.62	0.59	0.71	0.43
Job loss			0.36	0.23	0.43	0.19
Constant	−1.40	0.46	2.20	0.84	1.59	0.55
−2 Log L	884.93		714.49		1001.28	
Chi-square	55.5, 11 df		226.0, 18 df		295.5, 12 df	
Person-years	1419		1419		2271	
N of spells	249		249		288	

Table B.7 Cumulative Proportion Exiting Welfare by Family Background Characteristics

Years of Receipt	Parents' Education		Mother a Teen Mother	
	< H.S.	≥ H.S.	Yes	No
1	0.30	0.39	0.28	0.40
2	0.47	0.58	0.45	0.58
3	0.55	0.61	0.53	0.61
4	0.58	0.66	0.57	0.65
5	0.63	0.69	0.63	0.66
6	0.63	0.77	0.67	0.66
7	0.67	0.77	0.70	0.69
8	0.69	0.77	0.72	0.70
9	0.71	0.81	0.74	0.73
10+	0.95	0.95	0.96	0.90
N	192	70	174	89

Years of Receipt	Parents' Welfare Receipt		Family Structure in Adolescence	
	Yes	No	Single Parent	Two Parents
1	0.28	0.35	0.28	0.34
2	0.48	0.52	0.43	0.51
3	0.56	0.57	0.49	0.57
4	0.60	0.63	0.52	0.62
5	0.63	0.67	0.55	0.68
6	0.63	0.70	0.59	0.70
7	0.66	0.73	0.59	0.72
8	0.68	0.75	0.59	0.76
9	0.71	0.77	0.61	0.79
10+	0.98	0.93	0.87	0.96
N	78	193	93	152

Table B.8 Cumulative Proportion Exiting Welfare by Individual Characteristics at Time of Pregnancy

Years of Reciept	Age at First Pregnancy**		Married at First Birth**	
	<16	16+	No	Yes
1	0.24	0.37	0.32	0.40
2	0.37	0.56	0.47	0.67
3	0.42	0.62	0.53	0.73
4	0.47	0.67	0.57	0.82
5	0.49	0.73	0.62	0.84
6	0.50	0.76	0.65	0.84
7	0.54	0.78	0.68	0.87
8	0.59	0.78	0.69	0.89
9	0.61	0.81	0.72	0.91
10+	0.92	0.95	0.93	0.97
N	80	215	234	61

Years of Receipt	Educational Aspirations**		At Grade Level*	
	Low	High	No	Yes
1	0.29	0.40	0.27	0.36
2	0.45	0.60	0.41	0.54
3	0.52	0.64	0.51	0.59
4	0.57	0.69	0.55	0.65
5	0.61	0.74	0.59	0.69
6	0.63	0.77	0.60	0.72
7	0.66	0.79	0.62	0.75
8	0.68	0.80	0.63	0.77
9	0.72	0.81	0.63	0.80
10+	0.90	0.98	0.91	0.95
N	176	119	78	217

*Differences significant at the .05 level.
**Differences significant at the .01 level.

Table B.9   Parameter Estimates of the Probability of Welfare Exit

Explanatory Variables	1 b	1 SE	2 b	2 SE	3 b	3 SE
Duration:						
year 1	0.98	0.19	1.12	0.22	1.22	0.19
year 2	0.79	0.23	1.00	0.25	1.02	0.22
>2 years	—	—	—	—	—	—
First spell	−0.21	0.21	0.57	0.26	0.45	0.21
Parental education ≥ H.S.	0.09	0.21	−0.02	0.22		
Mother a teen mother	0.05	0.19	0.07	0.20		
Two parent household	0.14	0.20	0.14	0.20		
Parents receive welfare	0.04	0.19	0.14	0.20		
< 16 at first pregnancy	−0.31	0.19	−0.14	0.21		
High education aspirations	0.31	0.18	0.03	0.19	0.06	0.16
At grade level	0.20	0.21	0.05	0.22		
Married at first birth	0.33	0.31	0.24	0.33	0.60	0.20
Using birth control, T2	0.24	0.18	0.12	0.19		
< 20 years old			−0.51	0.32	−0.42	0.26
Education:						
< high school			—	—	—	—
high school			0.69	0.23	0.62	0.19
> high school			0.82	0.24	0.84	0.20
Preschool children			−0.63	0.23	−0.54	0.19
Female head			−0.28	0.22	−0.29	0.18
Cumulative work experience			0.03	0.02	0.04	0.02
OBRA			0.06	0.26	0.09	0.22
Unemployment rate			−0.09	0.07	−0.11	0.06
Constant	−2.89	0.44	−2.15	0.66	−2.20	0.46
−2 Log L	956.51		908.74		1273.13	
Chi-Square	49.4, 12 df		97.2, 20 df		135.9, 13 df	
Person years	1278		1278		1711	
N of spells	220		220		295	

Table B.10 Cumulative Proportion Returning to Welfare by Family Background Characteristics

Years Since Welfare Exit	Parents' Education		Mother a Teen Mother	
	< H.S.	≥ H.S.	Yes	No
1	0.08	0.09	0.10	0.06
2	0.15	0.16	0.15	0.16
3	0.23	0.18	0.22	0.22
4	0.26	0.27	0.25	0.29
5	0.27	0.29	0.26	0.30
6	0.29	0.34	0.30	0.32
7	0.32	0.34	0.31	0.36
8	0.35	0.39	0.35	0.38
9	0.37	0.41	0.38	0.40
10+	0.51	0.51	0.53	0.48
N	157	60	145	73

Years Since Welfare Exit	Parents' Welfare Receipt		Family Structure in Adolescence	
	Yes	No	Single Parent	Two Parents
1	0.14	0.05	0.10	0.08
2	0.19	0.12	0.12	0.18
3	0.28	0.18	0.20	0.21
4	0.32	0.24	0.22	0.29
5	0.34	0.25	0.23	0.30
6	0.36	0.28	0.27	0.32
7	0.38	0.30	0.31	0.33
8	0.38	0.34	0.34	0.35
9	0.38	0.36	0.34	0.38
10+	0.53	0.50	0.42	0.48
N	67	161	70	131

160

Table B.11   Cumulative Proportion Returning to Welfare by Individual
Characteristics at Time of Pregnancy

Years Since Welfare Exit	Age at First Pregnancy		Married at First Birth	
	<16	**16+**	**No**	**Yes**
1	0.08	0.08	0.07	0.11
2	0.15	0.15	0.15	0.15
3	0.19	0.22	0.20	0.28
4	0.21	0.28	0.25	0.31
5	0.21	0.29	0.26	0.33
6	0.26	0.32	0.29	0.33
7	0.26	0.34	0.31	0.33
8	0.34	0.35	0.35	0.33
9	0.37	0.37	0.36	0.40
10+	0.46	0.53	0.47	0.67
N	65	181	193	53

Years Since Welfare Exit	Educational Aspirations		At Grade Level	
	Low	**High**	**No**	**Yes**
1	0.08	0.09	0.08	0.08
2	0.18	0.11	0.14	0.15
3	0.26	0.16	0.24	0.21
4	0.31	0.20	0.29	0.26
5	0.32	0.21	0.29	0.27
6	0.34	0.25	0.29	0.31
7	0.35	0.27	0.31	0.32
8	0.36	0.33	0.34	0.35
9	0.39	0.34	0.38	0.37
10+	0.57	0.42	0.50	0.51
N	141	105	64	182

Table B.12 Parameter Estimates of the Probability of Welfare Return by Exit Route

Explanatory Variables	All Exits		Work Exits		Marriage/ Cohab & Other Exits	
	b	**SE**	**b**	**SE**	**b**	**SE**
Duration:						
year 1	0.66	0.31	0.01	0.42	1.10	0.44
year 2	0.38	0.34	0.15	0.40	0.16	0.60
year 3	0.64	0.33	—	—	—	—
> 3 years	—	—	—	—	—	—
At welfare exit:						
< 20 years old	0.12	0.29	0.15	0.37	0.18	0.50
3 or more children	0.32	0.11	0.54	0.14	0.01	0.18
Education:						
less than high school	—	—	—	—	—	—
high school graduate	−0.37	0.29	−0.19	0.39	−0.55	0.45
post-secondary	−0.34	0.27	−0.45	0.34	0.06	0.45
Female head	0.62	0.23	0.77	0.30	0.54	0.44
Marriage/Cohab. breakup	0.66	0.25	0.52	0.35	0.77	0.37
Job loss	1.32	0.22	1.58	0.30	1.20	0.36
Unemployment rate	0.04	0.07	−0.02	0.09	0.14	0.12
Constant	−4.87	0.62	−4.99	0.82	−4.69	0.96
−2 Log L	670.00		398.35		260.57	
Chi-Square	73.6, 11 df		56.2, 10 df		26.1, 10 df	
Person-years	2037		1363		674	
N of spells	246		154		92	

Table B.13   Parameter Estimates of the Transition to Work by Whether Work Results in Welfare Exit(standard errors in parentheses)

Explanatory Variables	Work & exit vs. no work		Work & no exit vs. no work		Work & exit vs. work & no exit	
	1	2	1	2	1	2
Duration:						
year 1	.80	1.04	−.31	−.22	1.11	1.26
	(.35)	(.38)	(.26)	(.28)	(.42)	(.45)
year 2	.84	1.00	−.40	−.29	1.24	1.29
	(.39)	(.42)	(.31)	(.33)	(.47)	(.51)
year 3	.43	.48	−.33	−.25	.77	.73
	(.49)	(.51)	(.36)	(.37)	(.58)	(.61)
year 4+	—	—	—	—	—	—
First spell	−.14	.60	.80	1.04	−.93	−.44
	(.38)	(.46)	(.42)	(.47)	(.55)	(.63)
Parents received welfare	−.45	−.32	.35	.37	−.80	−.69
	(.33)	(.35)	(.23)	(.23)	(.38)	(.40)
<16 at first pregnancy	−.80	−.34	−.10	.12	−.70	−.46
	(.31)	(.33)	(.22)	(.24)	(.7)	(.39)
High educational aspirations	.29	−.20	.41	.22	−.12	−.42
	(.28)	(.31)	(.25)	(.26)	(.35)	(.38)
At grade level	.65	.60	.36	.38	.29	.22
	(.31)	(.33)	(.24)	(.25)	(.38)	(.40)
Married at spell beginning	.02	.27	.10	.25	−.08	.02
	(.31)	(.34)	(.26)	(.27)	(.38)	(.41)
In school at spell beginning	.26	.65	−.11	−.07	.37	.72
	(.31)	(.35)	(.24)	(.25)	(.38)	(.41)
Previous work experience		−1.41		−.13		−1.28
		(.42)		(.26)		(.48)
Graduate high school		1.05		.24		.81
		(.31)		(.26)		(.38)
3 or more children		−1.05		−.74		−.31
		(.42)		(.29)		(.49)
Marry or cohabit		.53		.69		1.22
		(.37)		(.46)		(.56)
Age		.12		.05		.07
		(.47)		(.38)		(.06)
OBRA legislation		−.23		−.23		−.001
		(.53)		(.41)		(.64)
Rise in unemployment rate		−.27		−.17		−.10
		(.27)		(.22)		(.33)
Constant	−3.13	−6.74	−2.90	−4.14	−.23	−2.60
	(.51)	(1.45)	(.48)	(1.16)	(.68)	(1.75)
Log likelihood	−525.08	−501.61				
d.f.	20	34				
Person-years	902	902				
N of spells	346	346				

163

Table B.14 Parameter Estimates of the Probability of Welfare Exit Among Women Who Combine Work and Welfare

Explanatory variables	1		2	
	b	**SE**	**b**	**SE**
Duration of receipt:				
year 1	.76	.32	1.31	.36
year 2	.64	.36	1.09	.39
year 3	−.07	.54	.39	.56
year 4+	—		—	
First spell	−.42	.31	.15	.34
<16 at first pregnancy	−.48	.27	−.33	.29
High educational aspirations	.43	.23	.16	.25
At grade level in school	.48	.29	.31	.31
Married at spell beginning	.47	.25	.42	.26
3+ children at spell beginning	−.14	.34	−.08	.36
Cumulative work experience			.08	.04
Graduate high school			.56	.26
Preschool children present			−.56	.27
Marry or cohabit			.81	.34
OBRA legislation			−.08	.34
Rise in unemployment rate			−.10	.24
constant	−2.36	.50	−3.61	.71
Log likelihood	−499.7		−473.3	
d.f.	9		15	
person-years	607		607	
N of spells	106		106	

Notes

Chapter 1

1. AFDC is the primary social welfare program that provides cash assistance to poor families with children, the majority of whom are headed by single parents.

2. See chap. 1 of the National Academy of Sciences report prepared by the Panel on Adolescent Pregnancy and Childbearing (Hayes 1987), or Furstenberg, Brooks-Gunn, and Morgan (1987, 1–6) for a description of the various demographic and social processes that have occurred over the past three decades, altering the composition of adolescent childbearing to be predominately out of wedlock.

3. Between 1986 and 1991 the teenage birth rate rose by 25 percent. In 1992 this increase ceased, and tiny declines occurred in 1992 and 1993. Although the decline was small, it occurred in nearly every state and among black and white teens. It is too soon to tell whether this slight decline will continue as a sustained downturn in teenage fertility (Moore and Snyder 1996).

4. Bill Moyers's CBS television documentary "The Vanishing Family: Crisis in Black America" aired January 23, 1986.

5. The federal government adopted an official definition of poverty after the declaration of the War on Poverty. The federal government's official measure of poverty compares a family's or an individual's money income during a calendar year with an appropriate income threshold for that family or individual. If a family's total reported income during the previous calendar year falls below this threshold, then all persons in the family are classified as poor. The cutoffs provide an "absolute" measure of poverty that specifies in dollar terms the income necessary to provide minimally adequate levels of consumption. The thresholds are adjusted for household size, the age of the head of the household, and the number of children under age eighteen, and are updated yearly by change in the consumer price index (Danziger and Weinberg 1994). See Ruggles (1990) and Citro and Michael (1995) for further discussion of poverty measurement issues.

6. See, for instance, Greenstein (1985, 12–17); Kuttner (1984, 34–35); Ellwood and Summers (1986, 78–105); Jencks (1985, 41–49); Danziger and Gottschalk (1985, 32–38).

7. Italics in the original.

8. Before OBRA, the first thirty dollars of earnings, one-third of the remainder, and all work expenses were disregarded for the purpose of calculating AFDC benefits. OBRA limited work expenses to seventy-five dollars per month and allowed the "thirty and a third" to be disregarded for only the first four months of a new job. Families with a gross

income greater than 150 percent of the state's standard of need were denied eligibility for benefits, whatever their net income (Bane and Ellwood 1994).

9. The FSA includes four major components: stricter enforcement of child support, a JOBS program (work requirement), transitional child-care services, and transitional medicaid coverage for JOBS participants. The work requirement is generally defined to mean compulsory participation by all welfare mothers with children over age three in work-related activities than can include education, training, job search, and community work experience (U.S. Congress 1989).

In the 1990s a number of states have imposed a "family cap" on welfare mothers whereby additional welfare benefits are denied to women who have additional children while on welfare. New Jersey was the first state to add this limitation to their state welfare policy in 1992, to reduce welfare costs and hopefully deter subsequent nonmarital births in the welfare population.

10. Their conclusion is disputed by others. See Hoffman, Foster, and Furstenberg 1993a, 1993b.

11. They also find that teenage childbearing increases labor market activity over time. As the women age, the teen mothers work more hours and have higher earnings than the teens who delay childbearing (Hotz, McElroy, and Sanders 1995).

12. Exceptions include evaluations of the Teenage Parent Demonstration, an intervention program for teen parents on AFDC, by Mathematica Policy Research (see Gleason, Ranfarajan, and Schochet 1994; Maynard 1993).

13. New York Times, Thursday, March 23, 1989.

Chapter 2

1. For instance, the Panel Study of Income Dynamics (PSID) had a 50 percent response rate at its twenty-year follow-up interview (Survey Research Center 1989, 3).

2. For more information on this recording technique see Furstenberg, Brooks-Gunn, and Morgan (1987, 22–25, appendix A, p. 157) and Freedman et al. (1988).

3. For further discussion of monthly versus yearly data on welfare receipt as units of observation see Bane and Ellwood (1994, 30–33) and Harris (1993).

4. While all of the Baltimore mothers were age eighteen or younger when they became pregnant, some had turned nineteen by the time of the birth.

5. See Zinn and Sarri (1984) for a review of studies examining the impact of OBRA on working welfare recipients.

6. Cohabitation is defined as a relationship in which the mother lives with a male partner in the same household for a period of at least six months.

Chapter 3

1. Women still on welfare by the end of the study did not necessarily enter welfare at the time of the first birth. Spells of welfare can begin at any time throughout the twenty-year study period.

2. I derived the cumulative probability distribution from the conditional exit probabilities reported by Bane and Ellwood (1994, table 2.1, p. 32).

3. Note that the estimate of cumulative total years of welfare receipt is truncated by the end of the study period for those women currently in a spell of welfare at the twenty-year follow-up, as is exposure time for subsequent receipt; therefore the estimates are biased downward.

4. The PSID distribution is projected from the rates of welfare exit and reentry observed among single mothers in the PSID during the years 1968–88 and thus are not exactly the same as the distribution for the Baltimore mothers (see Bane and Ellwood 1994, 39–40, 173–77).

5. The AFDC-UP program provides benefits to two-parent families with children under eighteen, where one parent is unemployed. Benefits are based on the number of children in the household and the income level of the parent(s). About half the states, including Maryland, had AFDC-UP programs during the time period of the Baltimore Study.

Chapter 4

1. Women are eligible for AFDC when they are pregnant; however, recording of welfare receipt in the Baltimore data begins with the year of birth. For the adolescents who received welfare during pregnancy, the length of their first welfare spell may be too short, but this bias is minimal. By the time the teenager realized she was pregnant and applied for AFDC, it was probably late in her pregnancy and close to the time of first birth. It is unlikely that I will miss any welfare receipt; that is, it is unlikely that any teenagers who received welfare during pregnancy left by the time of first birth.

2. The risk set of 246 is a spell risk set in which women who have multiple spells of receipt are represented more than once.

3. I recognize that this procedure is somewhat limited in that the occurrence of concurrent events, such as a birth and job loss, are not classified but are represented within one of the mutually exclusive categories. Decisions for the priority of various events over others were based on the relevance of each event with respect to the economic status of the young mother. This approach is for descriptive purposes only, as

the importance and relative impact of concurrent events in precipitating welfare entry is examined in the multivariate hazard model of welfare entry (see table 4.3).

4. Note that initial spells can begin later than return spells. Women can experience an initial spell of welfare any time during the twenty-year study period, and some women do have their first spell in the mid-1980s, long after the women who entered welfare in the same year as the study birth have completed those spells and possibly had repeat spells.

5. This is the interpretation of an odds ratio for a dichotomous categorical independent variable. For continuous variables, an odds ratio indicates the chances of welfare entry for a one-unit increase in the level of the independent variable.

6. More formally, a significance level of .01 indicates that there is a one-in-a-hundred chance that the null hypothesis is true, where the null hypothesis states that the effect=0.

Chapter 5

1. Exceptions to studies concentrating on female-headed households are Coe's (1979) study, which examined welfare transitions among one- and two-adult families for the years 1973–76 in the PSID, and Rank (1986, 1994), who compared welfare patterns among female-headed households with children, married couples, and single households using caseload data from the state of Wisconsin during the early 1980s.

2. If a woman married or entered a cohabiting relationship and began a new job at the same time that she left welfare, marriage or cohabitation would be given priority as the ending event that facilitated welfare exit and the ending would be coded as a marriage exit.

3. Bane and Ellwood (1983, 1994) and Ellwood (1986) define "work exits" differently from the studies cited, which use work status around the time of welfare exit to classify work exits. Because Bane and Ellwood use the annual data on welfare receipt, they compare the annual earnings of the single mother on welfare to see if an increase in earnings occurs in the year of welfare exit. Earnings reports probably underestimate the level of work activity among welfare recipients, an issue discussed further in chaps. 7 and 8 (also see Edin and Jencks 1992; Harris 1993).

Chapter 6

1. The exceptions, of course, include evaluation research on welfare-to-work programs through the social experiments conducted by the Manpower Demonstration Research Corporation (see Friedlander and Burtless 1995; Gueron and Pauly 1991).

2. These return patterns are slightly different from those reported for all single mothers in the PSID by Bane and Ellwood (1994). Single mothers in the PSID return to welfare more rapidly than the Baltimore mothers. Within two years of welfare exit, 23 percent of

the PSID single mothers had returned to welfare compared to 15 percent among the Baltimore mothers. The Baltimore mothers, however, have higher return rates in the later durations since welfare exit and they cumulate more returns over time. Within seven years from welfare exit, about a third of the Baltimore mothers and the single mothers in the PSID have returned to welfare. Overall, fewer single mothers experience repeat dependency—35 percent compared to 50 percent of the Baltimore mothers.

3. Marriage and cohabitation exits were collapsed into one category because of the small number of these spell-ending types. Of the fifty-one exits in this category, thirty-one occurred through marriage and twenty through a live-in relationship that has lasted more than six months.

4. Even in models without the effects of marital and cohabitation breakup and job loss, education and age are not significant and thus do not have indirect effects on the probability of welfare return either.

5. The reference category includes women who remain in a marriage or a relationship and women who are not in a relationship or marriage. This effect captures the actual event of relationship breakup relative to all those who do not experience the event regardless of their relationship status.

Chapter 7

1. When welfare recipients work, benefits are taxed at a rate of 67 percent during the first four months of employment, and then at a rate of 100 percent beyond four months.

2. In 1967 Congress established the Work Incentive (WIN) program, which required employable welfare parents with children over the age of six to register for work and other job-related services. Although some form of work incentives remained in the system until 1981, the WIN program received relatively low funding (Levitan and Shapiro 1987).

3. Married women were eligible through the AFDC-UP provision. The break-even income is the income above which families are no longer eligible for AFDC, set by each state. The break-even income typically equals the state maximum AFDC benefit plus work expenses and is far below the poverty line. For instance, in 1994 the poverty line for a family of three with two children was $11,940, amounting to a monthly income of $995. The maximum AFDC grant for the median state was $366.00 a month and the break-even income was $456 a month, or about 46 percent of poverty (U.S. House of Representatives 1994).

Appendix B

1. While all women are followed for twenty years following their first birth, the small number of women whose first births occurred in 1966 and 1967 are followed for twenty-

two and twenty-one years, respectively, since the twenty-year follow-up occurred in 1987.

2. All model specification is based on exploratory analysis (Carroll 1983; Yamaguchi 1991). Exploratory analysis of the hazard function for each transition analyzed in this research was performed to test for time dependence of the hazard rate and to examine differences in the hazard function by spell number and by time-invariant characteristics of the women across time.

Bibliography

Abrahamse, Allan F., Peter A. Morrison, and Linda J. Waite. 1988. "Beyond Stereotypes: Who Becomes a Single Teenage Mother?" Paper No. R-3489-HHS/NICHD. Santa Monica: Rand Corporation.

Adams, Gina. 1987. "The Dynamics of Welfare Recipiency among Adolescent Mothers." Washington, D.C.: Congressional Budget Office.

Adams, Terry K., Greg J. Duncan, and Willard L. Rodgers. 1988. "The Persistence of Urban Poverty." In *Quiet Riots: Race and Poverty in the United States,* ed. Fred R. Harris and Roger W. Wilkins, 78–99. New York: Pantheon Books.

Allison, Paul D. 1982. "Discrete-Time Methods for the Analysis of Event Histories." *Sociological Methodology* 13:61–98.

———. 1984. *Event History Analysis: Regression for Longitudinal Event Data.* Sage University Papers: Quantitative Applications in the Social Sciences no. 07–046. Beverly Hills: Sage.

Anderson, Elijah. 1989. "Sex Codes and Family Life among Poor Inner-City Youths." *Annals of the American Academy of Political and Social Science* 501:59–78.

———. 1990. *Streetwise: Race, Class, and Change in an Urban Community.* Chicago: University of Chicago Press.

Auletta, Ken. 1982. *The Underclass.* New York: Random House.

Bachrach, Christine A. 1986. "Adoption Plans, Adopted Children, and Adoptive Mothers." *Journal of Marriage and the Family,* 48:243–53.

Bachrach, Christine A., and Karen Carver. 1992. *Outcomes of Early Childbearing: An Appraisal of Recent Evidence. Summary of a Conference.* [Bethesda, Md.]: National Institute of Child Health and Human Development.

Bane, Mary Jo, and David T. Ellwood. 1983. *The Dynamics of Dependence: The Routes to Self-Sufficiency.* Report prepared for Assistant Secretary for Planning and Evaluation, Office of Evaluation and Technical Analysis, Office of Income Security Policy, U.S. Department of Health and Human Services, Washington, D.C. Cambridge: Urban Systems Research and Engineering.

———. 1986. "Slipping into and out of Poverty: The Dynamics of Spells." *Journal of Human Resources* 21:1–23.

———. 1994. *Welfare Realities. From Rhetoric to Reform:* Cambridge: Harvard University Press.

Banfield, Edward C. [1970]. *The Unheavenly City: The Nature and Future of Our Urban Crisis.* Boston: Little, Brown.

Bassi, Laurie J. 1984. "Estimating the Effect of Training Programs with Non-random Selection." *Review of Economics and Statistics* 66:36–43.

Bassi, Laurie J., and Orley Ashenfelter. 1986. "The Effect of Direct Job Creation and Training Programs on Low-Skilled Workers." In *Fighting Poverty: What Works and What Doesn't,* ed. Sheldon H. Danziger and David H. Weinberg, 133–51. Cambridge: Harvard University Press.

Besharov, Douglas J. 1989. "Targeting Long-Term Welfare Recipients." In *Welfare Policy for the 1990s,* ed. Phoebe H. Cottingham and David T. Ellwood, 146–64. Cambridge: Harvard University Press.

Bianchi, Suzanne M. 1993. "Children of Poverty: Why Are They Poor?" In *Child Poverty and Public Policy,* ed. Judith A. Chafel, 91–125. Washington, D.C.: Urban Institute Press.

Bianchi, Suzanne M., and Daphne Spain. 1986. *American Women in Transition.* The Population of the United States in the 1980s. A Census Monograph Series. New York: Russell Sage Foundation for the National Committee for Research on the 1980 Census.

Billy, John O. G., Nancy S. Landale, and Steven D. McLaughlin. 1986. "The Effect of Marital Status at First Birth on Marital Dissolution among Adolescent Mothers." *Demography* 23:329–49.

Blank, Rebecca M. 1989. "Analyzing the Length of Welfare Spells." *Journal of Public Economics* 39:245–73.

————. 1994. "The Employment Strategy: Public Policies to Increase Work and Earnings." In *Confronting Poverty: Prescriptions for Change,* ed. Sheldon H. Danziger, Gary D. Sandefur, and Daniel H. Weinberg, 168–204. New York: Russell Sage Foundation; Cambridge: Harvard University Press.

Block, A. Harvey, and S. Dubin, eds. 1981. *Research on the Societal Consequences of Adolescent Childbearing: Welfare Costs at the Local Level.* Final report to National Institute of Child Health and Human Development. Washington, D.C.: Bokonon Systems.

Block, Fred L., Richard A. Cloward, Barbara Ehrenreich, and Frances Fox Piven. 1987. *The Mean Season: The Attack on the Welfare State.* New York: Pantheon Books.

Brooks-Gunn, Jeanne, Guang Guo, and Frank F. Furstenberg Jr. 1993. "Who Drops Out of and Who Continues beyond High School? A Twenty-Year Follow-up of Black Youth." *Journal of Adolescent Research* 3:271–94.

Brooks-Gunn, Jeanne and Frank F. Furstenberg, Jr. 1986. "The Children of Adolescent Mothers: Physical, Academic, and Psychological Outcomes." *Developmental Review* 7:224–251.

Bumpass, Larry L., Ronald R. Rindfuss, and Richard B. Janosik. 1978. "Age and Marital Status at First Birth and the Pace of Subsequent Fertility." *Demography* 15:75–86.

Burt, Martha R., with Frank S. Levy. 1987. "Estimates of Public Costs for Teenage Childbearing: A Review of Recent Studies and Estimates of 1985 Public Costs." In *Risking the Future: Adolescent Sexuality, Pregnancy, and Childbearing.* Vol. 2, *Working Papers and Statistical Appendixes,* ed. Sandra L. Hofferth and Cheryl D. Hayes. Washington, D.C.: National Academy Press, 264–93.

Burtless, Gary. 1994. "Public Spending on the Poor: Historical Trends and Economic Limits." In *Confronting Poverty: Prescriptions for Change,* ed. Sheldon H. Danziger, Gary D. Sandefur, and Daniel H. Weinberg, 51–84. New York: Russell Sage Foundation; Cambridge: Harvard University Press.

Burton, Linda M. 1990. "Teenage Childbearing as an Alternative Life-Course Strategy in Multigenerational Black Families." *Human Nature* 1:123–43.

Butler, Amy C. 1992. "The Changing Economic Consequences of Teenage Childbearing." *Social Service Review* 66:1–31.

Card, Josefina J., and Lauress L. Wise. 1978. "Teenage Mothers and Teenage Fathers: The Impact of Early Childbearing on the Parents' Personal and Professional Lives." *Family Planning Perspectives* 10:199–205.

Carroll, Glenn R. 1983. "Dynamic Analysis of Discrete Dependent Variables: A Didactic Essay." *Quality and Quantity* 17:425–60.

Center for Human Resource Research. 1995. *NLS Handbook 1995. The National Longitudinal Surveys.* Columbus: Center for Human Resource Research, Ohio State University.

Cherlin, Andrew J. 1992. *Marriage, Divorce, Remarriage.* Cambridge: Harvard University Press.

Chilman, Catherine S. 1983. *Adolescent Sexuality in a Changing American Society: Social and Psychological Perspectives for the Human Services Professions.* 2d ed. Wiley Series on Personality Processes, 0195–4008. New York: Wiley.

Citro, Constance F., and Robert T. Michael. 1995. *Measuring Poverty: A New Approach, Summary and Recommendations.* Panel on Poverty and Family Assistance: Concepts, Information Needs, and Measurement Methods. Committee on National Statistics. Commission on Behavioral and Social Sciences and Education. National Research Council. Washington, D.C.: National Academy Press.

Clark, Kenneth B. [1965]. *The Dark Ghetto: Dilemmas of Social Power.* New York: Harper and Row.

Coe, Richard D. 1979. "An Examination of the Dynamics of Food Stamp Use." In *Five Thousand American Families: Patterns of Economic Progress,* ed. Greg J. Duncan and James N. Morgan. Vol. 7, *Analyses of the First Ten Years of the Panel Study of Income Dynamics,* 183–268. Ann Arbor: Survey Research Center of the Institute for Social Research, University of Michigan.

Cottingham, Phoebe H., and David T. Ellwood. 1989. *Welfare Policy for the 1990s.* Cambridge: Harvard University Press.

Danziger, Sheldon H., and Peter Gottschalk. 1985. "The Poverty of Losing Ground." *Challenge Magazine* 28 (May–June): 32–38.

Danziger, Sheldon H., Robert Haveman, and Robert Plotnick. 1981. "How Income Transfer Programs Affect Work, Savings, and the Income Distribution." *Journal of Economic Literature* 18:975–1028.

Danziger, Sheldon H., Gary D. Sandefur, and Daniel H. Weinberg, eds. 1994. *Confronting Poverty: Prescription for Change.* New York: Russell Sage Foundation; Cambridge: Harvard University Press.

Danziger, Sheldon H., and Daniel H. Weinberg. 1994. "The Historical Record: Trends in Family Income, Inequality, and Poverty." In *Confronting Poverty: Prescription for Change,* ed. Sheldon H. Danziger, Gary D. Sandefur, and Daniel H. Weinberg, 18–50. New York: Russell Sage Foundation; Cambridge: Harvard University Press.

Dash, Leon. 1989. *When Children Want Children: The Urban Crisis of Teenage Childbearing.* New York: William Morrow.

Duncan, Greg J., with Richard D. Coe. 1984. *Years of Poverty, Years of Plenty: The Changing Economic Fortunes of American Workers and Families.* Ann Arbor: Survey Research Center, Institute for Social Research, University of Michigan.

Duncan, Greg J., Martha S. Hill, and Saul D. Hoffman. 1988. "Welfare Dependence within and across Generations." *Science* 239:467–71.

Duncan, Greg J., and Saul D. Hoffman. 1988. "The Use and Effects of Welfare: A Survey of Recent Evidence." *Social Service Review* 62:238–57.

———. 1990a. "Teenage Welfare Receipt and Subsequent Dependence among Black Adolescent Mothers." *Family Planning Perspectives* 22:16–20.

———. 1990b. "Welfare Benefits, Economic Opportunities, and Out-of-Wedlock Births among Black Teenage Girls." *Demography* 27:519–35.

———. 1991. "Teenage Underclass Behavior and Subsequent Poverty: Have the Rules Changed?" In *The Urban Underclass,* ed. Christopher Jencks and Paul E. Peterson, 155–74. Washington, D.C.: Brookings Institution.

Eberstadt, Nick. 1988. "Economic and Material Poverty in the U.S." *Public Interest* no. 90:50–65.

Edin, Kathryn, and Christopher Jencks. 1992. "Reforming Welfare." In *Rethinking Social Policy: Race, Poverty, and the Underclass,* ed. Christopher Jencks, 205–75. Cambridge: Harvard University Press.

Edin, Kathryn, and Laura Lein. 1996. *Making Ends Meet: How Single Mothers Survive Welfare and Low-Wage Work.* New York: Russell Sage Foundation.

Elder, Glen H., Jr. 1978. "Family History and the Life Course." In *Transitions: The Family and the Life Course in Historical Perspective,* ed. Tamara Hareven, 17–64. New York: Academic Press.

———. 1985. "Perspectives on the Life Course." In *Life Course Dynamics: Trajectories and Transitions, 1968–1980,* ed. Glen H. Elder Jr., 23–49. Ithaca, N.Y.: Cornell University Press.

Ellwood, David T. 1986. *Targeting "Would Be" Long-Term Recipients of AFDC.* Princeton: Mathematica Policy Research.

———. 1987. *Understanding Dependency: Choices, Confidence, or Culture?* Washington, D.C.: Income Security Policy-Research, Assistant Secretary for Planning and Evaluation, Office of the Secretary, U. S. Department of Health and Human Services.

———. 1988. *Poor Support: Poverty in the American Family.* New York: Basic Books.

Ellwood, David T., and Mary Jo Bane. 1985. "The Impact of AFDC on Family Structure and Living Arrangements." *Research in Labor Economics* 7:137–297.

Ellwood, David T., and Lawrence H. Summers. 1986. "Poverty in America: Is Welfare the Answer or the Problem?" In *Fighting Poverty: What Works and What Doesn't,* ed. Sheldon H. Danziger and Daniel H. Weinberg, 78–105. Cambridge: Harvard University Press.

Fitzgerald, John. 1991. "Welfare Durations and the Marriage Market: Evidence from the Survey of Income and Program Participation." *Journal of Human Resources* 26:454–561.

Freedman, Deborah S., Arlan Thornton, Donald Camburn, Duane Alwin, and Linda Young-DeMarco. 1988. "The Life History Calendar: A Technique for Collecting Retrospective Data." *Sociological Methodology* 18:37–68.

Freeman, Richard B. 1991. "Employment and Earnings of Disadvantaged Young Men in a Labor Shortage Economy." In *The Urban Underclass,* ed. Christopher Jencks and Paul E. Peterson, 103–21. Washington, D.C.: Brookings Institution.

Friedlander, Daniel, and Gary Burtless. 1995. *Five Years After: The Long-Term Effects of Welfare-to-Work Programs.* New York: Russell Sage Foundation.

Furstenberg, Frank F., Jr. 1976. *Unplanned Parenthood: The Social Consequences of Teenage Childbearing.* New York: Free Press.

———. 1981. "Implicating the Family: Teenage Parenthood and Kinship Involvement." In *Teenage Pregnancy in a Family Context: Implications for Policy,* ed. Theodora Ooms. Family Impact Seminar Series. Philadelphia: Temple University Press.

———. 1988. "The Teenage Marriage Controversy: Bringing Back the Shotgun Wedding." *Public Interest* 90 (Winter): 121–27.

Furstenberg, Frank F., Jr., with the assistance of Alisa Belzer, Colleen Davis, Judith A. Levine, Kristine Morrow, and Mary Washington. 1993. "How Families Manage Risk and Opportunity in Dangerous Neighborhoods." In *Sociology and the Public Agenda,* ed. William J. Wilson, 231–58. American Sociological Association Presidential Series. Newbury Park, Calif.: Sage.

Furstenberg, Frank F., Jr., Jeanne Brooks-Gunn, and S. Philip Morgan. 1987. *Adolescent Mothers in Later Life.* Human Development in Cultural and Historical Contexts. New York: Cambridge University Press.

Furstenberg, Frank F., Jr., and Albert G. Crawford. 1978. "Family Support: Helping Teenage Mothers to Cope." *Family Planning Perspectives* 10:322–33.

Furstenberg, Frank F., Jr., and Kathleen Mullan Harris. 1993. "When Fathers Matter/Why Fathers Matter: The Impact of Paternal Involvement on the Offspring of Adolescent Mothers." In *The Politics of Pregnancy: Adolescent Sexuality and Public Policy,* eds. Annette Lawson and Deborah L. Rhode, 189–215. New Haven, CT: Yale University Press.

Furstenberg, Frank F., Jr., Judith A. Levine, and Jeanne Brooks-Gunn. 1990. "The Children of Teenage Mothers: Patterns of Early Childbearing in Two Generations." *Family Planning Perspectives* 22:54–61.

Gans, Herbert J. [1962]. *Urban Villagers: Group and Class in the Life of Italian-Americans.* [New York]: Free Press of Glencoe.

Garfinkel, Irwin, and Sara S. McLanahan. 1986. *Single Mothers and Their Children.* The Changing Domestic Priorities Series. Washington, D.C.: Urban Institute Press.

Geronimus, Arline T. 1991. "Teenage Childbearing and Social and Reproductive Disadvantage: The Evolution of Complex Questions and the Demise of Simple Answers." *Family Relations* 40:463–71.

————. 1992. "Teenage Childbearing and Social Disadvantage: Unprotected Discourse." *Family Relations* 41:244–48.

Geronimus, Arline T., and Sanders Korenman. 1992. "The Socioeconomic Consequences of Teen Childbearing Reconsidered." *Quarterly Journal of Economics* 107:1187–214.

Gilder, George F. 1981. *Wealth and Poverty*. New York: Basic Books.

Gleason, Phil, Anu Ranfarajan, and Peter Schochet. 1994. "The Dynamics of AFDC Spells among Teenage Parents." Paper presented at the Annual Meeting of the Population Association of America, Miami, May 2–7.

Goodwin, Leonard. 1983. *Causes and Cures of Welfare: New Evidence on the Social Psychology of the Poor*. Lexington, Mass.: Lexington Books.

Gordon, Linda. 1994. *Pitied But Not Entitled: Single Mothers and the History of Welfare*. New York: The Free Press.

Gottschalk, Peter, Sara McLanahan,, and Gary D. Sandefur. 1994. "The Dynamics and Intergenerational Transmission of Poverty and Welfare Participation." In *Confronting Poverty: Prescription for Change,* ed. Sheldon H. Danziger, Gary D. Sandefur and Daniel H. Weinberg, 85–108. New York: Russell Sage Foundation; Cambridge: Harvard University Press.

Gottschalk, Peter, and Robert A. Moffitt. 1994. "Welfare Dependence: Concepts, Measures, and Trends." *American Economic Review* 84:38–42.

Greenstein, Robert. 1985. "Losing Faith in 'Losing Ground' — The Intellectual Mugging of the Great Society." *New Republic,* March 25, 12–17.

Gritz, R. Mark, and Thomas MaCurdy. 1991. "Welfare Entrances, Durations, and Exits: A Comparison of NLSY and PSID." Paper presented at the PSID [Panel Study of Income Dynamics] Event History Conference, Stanford, June 30–July 2.

Gueron, Judith M., and Edward Pauly, with Cameran M. Lougy. 1991. *From Welfare to Work*. New York: Russell Sage Foundation.

Haggstrom, Gus W., and Peter A. Morrison. 1979. "Consequences of Parenthood in Late Adolescence: Findings from the National Longitudinal Study of High School Seniors." Santa Monica: Rand.

Harrington, Michael. 1962. *The Other America: Poverty in the United States*. New York: Macmillan.

177

Harris, Kathleen Mullan. 1991. "Teenage Mothers and Welfare Dependency: Working off Welfare." *Journal of Family Issues* 12:492–518.

———. 1993. "Work and Welfare among Single Mothers in Poverty." *American Journal of Sociology* 99:317–52.

———. 1996. "Life after Welfare: Women, Work, and Repeat Dependency." *American Sociological Review* 61:407–26.

Harrison, Bennett. 1977. *Labor Market Structure and the Relationship between Work and Welfare.* Working Paper no. 50. [Cambridge, Mass.]: Joint Center for Urban Studies of MIT and Harvard University.

Haveman, Robert, and Barbara Wolfe. 1994. *Succeeding Generations.* New York: Russell Sage Foundation.

Hayes, Cheryl D., ed. 1987. *Risking the Future: Adolescent Sexuality, Pregnancy, and Childbearing.* Vol. 1. Washington, D.C.: National Academy Press.

Heclo, Hugh. 1994. "Poverty Politics." In *Confronting Poverty: Prescriptions for Change,* ed. Sheldon H. Danziger, Gary D. Sandefur, and Daniel H. Weinberg, 396–437. New York: Russell Sage Foundation; Cambridge: Harvard University Press.

Hofferth, Sandra L. 1987. "Social and Economic Consequences of Teenage Childbearing." In *Risking the Future: Adolescent Sexuality, Pregnancy, and Childbearing.* Vol. 2, *Working Papers and Statistical Appendixes,* ed. Sandra L. Hofferth and Cheryl D. Hayes, 123–44. Washington, D.C.: National Academy Press.

Hofferth, Sandra L., and Cheryl D. Hayes, eds. 1987. *Risking the Future: Adolescent Sexuality, Pregnancy, and Childbearing.* Vol. 2, *Working Papers and Statistical Appendixes.* Washington, D.C.: National Academy Press.

Hofferth, Sandra L., and Kristin A. Moore. 1979. "Early Childbearing and Later Economic Well-Being." *American Sociological Review* 44:784–815.

Hoffman, Saul D., E. Michael Foster, and Frank F. Furstenberg Jr. 1993a. "Reevaluating the Costs of Teenage Childbearing." *Demography* 30:1–13.

———. 1993b. "Reevaluating the Costs of Teenage Childbearing: Response to Geronimus and Korenman." *Demography* 30:291–96.

Hogan, Dennis P. 1978. "The Variable Order of Events in the Life Course." *American Sociological Review* 43:573–586.

Hogan, Dennis P., and Evelyn M. Kitagawa. 1985. "The Impact of Social Status, Family Structure, and Neighborhood on the Fertility of Black Adolescents." *American Journal of Sociology* 90:825–55.

Hotz, V. Joseph, Susan Williams McElroy, and Seth G. Sanders. 1995. "The Costs and Consequences of Teenage Childbearing for Mothers." In *Kids Having Kids: The Consequences and Costs of Teenage Childbearing in the United States*. Report of the Robin Hood Foundation (April).

Hotz, V. Joseph, Charles H. Mullin, and Seth G. Sanders. Forthcoming. "Bounding Causal Effects Using Contaminated Instrumental Variables: Analyzing the Effects of Teenage Childbearing Using a Natural Experiment." *Review of Economic Studies*.

Hutchens, Robert M. 1981. "Entry and Exit Transitions in a Government Transfer Program: The Case of Aid to Families with Dependent Children." *Journal of Human Resources* 16:217–37.

Jargowsky, Paul A., and Mary Jo Bane. 1991. "Ghetto Poverty in the United States, 1970–1980." In *The Urban Underclass*, ed. Christopher Jencks and Paul E. Peterson, 235–73. Washington, D.C.: Brookings Institution.

Jencks, Christopher. 1985. "How Poor Are the Poor?" Review of Charles Murray, *Losing Ground: American Social Policy, 1950–1980. New York Review of Books,* May 9, 1985, 41–49.

———. 1991. "Is the American Underclass Growing?" In *The Urban Underclass,* ed. Christopher Jencks and Paul E. Peterson, 28–100. Washington, D.C.: The Brookings Institution.

Jencks, Christopher, and Paul E. Peterson, eds. 1991. *The Urban Underclass.* Washington, D.C.: Brookings Institution.

Johnson, Clifford M. and Andrew M. Sum. 1987. *Declining Earnings of Young Men: Their Relation to Poverty, Teen Pregnancy, and Family Formation.* A Publication of the Adolescent Pregnancy Prevention Clearinghouse. Washington D.C.: Children's Defense Fund.

Kasarda, John D. 1985. "Urban Change and Minority Opportunities." In *The New Urban Reality,* ed. Paul E. Peterson, 41–47. Washington D.C.: Brookings Institution.

———. 1989. "Urban Industrial Transition and the Underclass." *Annals of the American Academy of Political and Social Science* 501:26–47.

Katz, Michael B. 1986. *In the Shadow of the Poorhouse: A Social History of Welfare in America.* New York: Basic Books.

———. 1989. *The Undeserving Poor: From the War on Poverty to the War on Welfare.* New York: Pantheon Books.

Kaus, Mickey. 1986. "The Work Ethic State: The Only Way to Break the Culture of Poverty." *New Republic,* July 7, 22–32.

Koo, Helen P., and Richard E. Bilsborrow, with the assistance of Harlene C. Gogan. 1979. *Multivariate Analyses of Effects of Age at First Birth: Results from the 1973 National Survey of Family Growth and 1975 Current Population Survey.* Final report to National Institute of Child Health and Human Development. Research Triangle Park, N.C.: Research Triangle Institute.

Kuttner, Robert. 1984. "A Flawed Case for Scrapping What's Left of the Great Society." *Washington Post Book World,* December 17, 34–35.

Ladner, Joyce A. 1971. *Tomorrow's Tomorrow: The Black Woman.* Garden City, N.Y.: Doubleday.

Lawson, Annette, and Deborah L. Rhode, eds. 1993. *The Politics of Pregnancy. Adolescent Sexuality and Public Policy.* New Haven: Yale University Press.

Lemann, Nicholas. 1986. "The Origins of the Underclass." *Atlantic Monthly,* June, 31–43, 47–55.

Levitan, Sar A., and Isaac Shapiro. 1987. *Working But Poor: America's Contradiction.* Baltimore: Johns Hopkins University Press.

Levy, Frank S. 1982. "The Structure of CETA Earnings Gains." Project report. Washington, D.C.: Urban Institute.

———. 1987. *Dollars and Dreams: The Changing American Income Distribution.* The Population of the United States in the 1980s. New York: Russell Sage Foundation for the National Committee for Research on the 1980 Census.

Levy, Frank S., and Richard J. Murnane. 1992. "U.S. Earnings Levels and Earnings Inequality: A Review of Recent Trends and Proposed Explanations." *Journal of Economic Literature* 30:1333–81.

Lewis, Oscar. [1966]. *La Vida: A Puerto Rican Family in the Culture of Poverty—San Juan and New York.* New York: Random House.

Lichter, Daniel T., Diane K. McLaughlin, George Kephart, and David J. Landry. 1992. "Race and the Retreat from Marriage: A Shortage of Marriageable Men?" *American Sociological Review* 57:781–99.

Luker, Kristin. 1991. "Dubious Conceptions: The Controversy over Teen Pregnancy." *American Prospect* 5:73–83.

Lundberg, Shelly, and Robert D. Plotnick. 1990. "Effects of State Welfare, Abortion and Family Planning Policies on Premarital Childbearing among White Adolescents." *Family Planning Perspectives* 22:246–51.

Mare, Robert D., and Christopher Winship. 1991. "Socioeconomic Change and the Decline of Marriage for Blacks and Whites." In *The Urban Underclass,* ed.

Christopher Jencks and Paul E. Peterson, 175–202. Washington, D.C.: The Brookings Institution.

Marini, Margaret Mooney. 1984. "Women's Educational Attainment and the Timing of Entry into Parenthood." *American Sociological Review* 49:491–511.

———. 1989. "Sex Differences in Earnings in the United States." *Annual Review of Sociology* 15:343–80.

Massey, Douglas S., and Nancy A. Denton. 1989. "Hypersegregation in U.S. Metropolitan Areas: Black and Hispanic Segregation along Five Dimensions." *Demography* 26:373–91.

———. 1993. *American Apartheid: Segregation and the Making of the Underclass.* Cambridge: Harvard University Press.

Maynard, Rebecca A. 1993. *Building Self-Sufficiency among Welfare-Dependent Teenage Parents: Lessons from the Teenage Parent Demonstration.* Princeton: Mathematica Policy Research.

McCarthy, James, and Jane Menken. 1979. "Marriage, Remarriage, Marital Disruption and Age at First Birth." *Family Planning Perspectives* 11:21–30.

McCrate, Elaine. 1990. "Labor Market Segmentation and Relative Black-White Teenage Birth Rates." *Review of Black Political Economy* 18(4):37–53.

———. 1992. "Expectations of Adult Wages and Teenage Childbearing." Paper presented at the annual meeting of the Population Association of America, Denver, April 30–May 2.

McFate, Katherine, Roger Lawson, and William Julius Wilson, eds. 1995. *Poverty, Inequality, and the Future of Social Policy: Western States in the New World Order.* New York: Russell Sage Foundation.

McLanahan, Sara S. 1988. "Family Structure and Dependency: Early Transitions to Female Household Headship." *Demography* 25:1–16.

McLanahan, Sara S., and Karen Booth. 1989. "Mother-Only Families: Problems, Prospects, and Politics." *Journal of Marriage and the Family* 51:557–80.

McLanahan, Sara S., and Larry L. Bumpass. 1988. "Intergenerational Consequences of Family Disruption." *American Journal of Sociology* 94:130–52.

McLanahan, Sara S., and Irwin Garfinkel. 1989. "Single Mothers, the Underclass, and Social Policy." *Annals of the American Academy of Political and Social Science* 501:92–104.

McLanahan, Sara S., and Gary D. Sandefur. 1994. *Growing Up with a Single Parent: What Hurts, What Helps.* Cambridge: Harvard University Press.

Mead, Lawrence M. 1986. *Beyond Entitlement: The Social Obligations of Citizenship.* New York: Free Press.

———. 1992. *The New Politics of Poverty: The Nonworking Poor in America.* New York: Basic Books.

Michael, Robert T., and Nancy Brandon Tuma. 1985. "Entry into Marriage and Parenthood by Young Men and Women: The Influence of Family Background." *Demography* 22:515–44.

Millman, Sara R., and Gerry E. Hendershot. 1980. "Early Fertility and Lifetime Fertility." *Family Planning Perspectives* 12:139–40, 145–49.

Moen, Phyllis. 1985. "Continuities and Discontinuities in Women's Labor Force Activity." In *Life Course Dynamics: Trajectories and Transitions, 1968–1980,* ed. Glen H. Elder Jr., 113–55. Ithaca: Cornell University Press.

———. 1992. *Women's Two Roles: A Contemporary Dilemma.* New York: Auburn House.

Moffitt, Robert. 1983. "An Economic Model of Welfare Stigma." *American Economic Review* 73:1023–35.

———. 1992. "Incentive Effects of the U.S. Welfare System: A Review." *Journal of Economic Literature* 30:1–61.

Moore, Kristin A. 1978. "Teenage Childbirth and Welfare Dependency." *Family Planning Perspectives* 10:233–35.

Moore, Kristin A., and Martha R. Burt. 1982. *Private Crisis, Public Cost: Policy Perspectives on Teenage Childbearing.* Washington, D.C.: Urban Institute Press.

Moore, Kristin A., David E. Myers, Donna Ruane Morrison, Christine Winquist Nord, Brett Brown, and Barry Edmonston. 1993. "Age at First Childbirth and Later Poverty." *Journal of Research on Adolescence* 3:393–422.

Moore, Kristin A., Margaret C. Simms, and Charles L. Betsey. 1989. *Choice and Circumstance: Racial Differences in Adolescent Sexuality and Fertility.* New Brunswick, N.J.: Transaction Books.

Moore, Kristin A., and Nancy O. Snyder. 1996. *Facts at a Glance* (January). Washington, D.C.: Child Trends.

Moore, Kristin A., Nancy O. Snyder, and Dana Glei. 1995. *Facts at a Glance* (February). Washington, D.C.: Child Trends, Inc.

Moore, Kristin A., and Linda J. Waite. 1981. "Marital Dissolution, Early Motherhood, and Early Marriage." *Social Forces* 60:20–40.

Moore, Kristin A., Dee Ann L. Wenk, Sandra L. Hofferth, and Cheryl D. Hayes, eds. 1987. "Statistical Appendix: Trends in Adolescent Sexual and Fertility Behavior." In *Risking the Future: Adolescent Sexuality, Pregnancy, and Childbearing.* Vol. 2, *Working Papers and Statistical Appendixes,* ed. Sandra L. Hofferth and Cheryl D. Hayes, A-1/353–1-168/520. Washington, D.C.: National Academy Press.

Mott, Frank L. 1986. "The Pace of Repeated Childbearing among Young American Mothers." *Family Planning Perspectives* 18:5–12.

Mott, Frank L., and William Marsiglio. 1985. "Early Childbearing and Completion of High School." *Family Planning Perspectives* 17:234–37.

Moynihan, Daniel Patrick. 1967. "The Negro Family: The Case for National Action." In *The Moynihan Report and the Politics of Controversy; A Trans-actional Social Sciences and Public Policy Report,* ed. Lee Rainwater and William L. Yancey, 39–124. Cambridge: MIT Press.

———. 1986. *Family and Nation.* The Godkin Lectures, Harvard University, 1985. San Diego: Harcourt Brace Jovanovich.

Murray, Charles A. 1984. *Losing Ground: American Social Policy, 1950–1980.* New York: Basic Books.

———. 1993. "The Coming White Underclass." *Wall Street Journal,* October 29.

Namboodiri, N. Krishnan, and C. M. Suchindran. 1987. *Life Table Techniques and Their Applications.* In *Studies in Population,* ed. H. H. Winsborough. Orlando: Academic Press.

Nathanson, Constance A. 1991. *Dangerous Passage: The Social Control of Women's Sexuality in Adolescence.* Health, Society, and Policy. Philadelphia: Temple University Press.

O'Connell, Martin, and Carolyn C. Rogers. 1984. "Out-of-Wedlock Births, Premarital Pregnancies, and Their Effect on Family Formation and Dissolution." *Family Planning Perspectives* 16:157–62.

Oliker, Stacey J. 1995. "Proximate Contexts of Workfare and Work: A Framework for Studying Poor Women's Economic Choices." *Sociological Quarterly* 36:251–72.

Olsen, Randall, and George Farkas. 1989. "Endogenous Covariates in Duration Models and the Effect of Adolescent Childbirth on Schooling." *Journal of Human Resources* 24:39–53.

O'Neill, June A., Laurie J. Bassi, and Douglas A. Wolf. 1987. "The Duration of Welfare Spells." *Review of Economics and Statistics* 69:241–49.

O'Neill, June A., Douglas A. Wolf, Laurie J. Bassi, and Michael T. Hannan. 1984. "An Analysis of Time on Welfare." No. PB84–225713. Washington, D.C.: Urban Institute.

Pavetti, LaDonna A. 1993. "The Dynamics of Welfare and Work: Exploring the Process by Which Young Women Work Their Way off Welfare." Ph.D. diss., Harvard University.

Pearce, Diana. 1979. "Women, Work, and Welfare: The Feminization of Poverty." In *Working Women and Families,* ed. Karen Wolk Feinstein, 103–24. Sage Yearbooks in Women's Policy Studies. Vol. 4. Beverly Hills: Sage.

———. 1983. "The Feminization of Ghetto Poverty." *Society* 21 (November–December): 70–74.

Piven, Frances Fox, and Richard Cloward. 1971. *Regulating the Poor: The Functions of Pubic Welfare.* New York: Pantheon.

Plotnick, Robert D. 1983. "Turnover in the AFDC Population: An Event History Analysis." *Journal of Human Resources* 18:65–81.

———. 1990. "Welfare and Out-of-Wedlock Childbearing: Evidence from the 1980s." *Journal of Marriage and the Family* 52:735–46.

Presser, Harriet B. 1980. "Social Consequences of Teenage Childbearing." In *Adolescent Pregnancy and Childbearing: Findings from Research,* ed. Catherine S. Chilman. NIH Publication no. 81–2077. [Bethesda, Md.]: National Institutes of Health, Public Health Service, U.S. Department of Health and Human Services.

Presser, Harriet B., and Wendy Baldwin. 1980. "Child Care as a Constraint on Employment: Prevalence, Correlates, and Bearing on the Work and Fertility Nexus." *American Journal of Sociology* 85:1202–13.

Rank, Mark Robert. 1986. "Family Structure and the Process of Exiting from Welfare." *Journal of Marriage and the Family* 48:607–18.

———. 1994. *Living on the Edge: The Realities of Welfare in America.* New York: Columbia University Press.

Rawlings, Steve W. 1994. "Household and Family Characteristics: March 1993." *Current Population Reports,* Series P20–477. Washington, D.C.: Bureau of the Census, Economics and Statistics Administration, U.S. Department of Commerce.

Rein, Martin, and Lee Rainwater. 1978. "Patterns of Welfare Use." *Social Service Review* 52:511–34.

Reischauer, Robert Danton. 1989. "The Welfare Reform Legislation: Directions for the Future." In *Welfare Policy for the 1990s,* ed. Phoebe H. Cottingham and David T. Ellwood, 10–40. Cambridge: Harvard University Press.

Ribar, David C. 1994a. "The Socioeconomic Consequences of Young Women's Childbearing: Reconciling Disparate Evidence." Working Paper no. 4-94-1. University Park, Penn.: Department of Economics and Population Research Institute, Pennsylvania State University.

————. 1994b. "Teenage Fertility and High School Completion." *Review of Economics and Statistics* 76:413:24.

Rindfuss, Ronald R., Craig St. John, and Larry L. Bumpass. 1984. "Education and the Timing of Motherhood: Disentangling Causation." *Journal of Marriage and the Family* 46:981–84.

Rudd, Nancy M., Patrick C. McKenry, and Myungkyun Nah. 1990. "Welfare Receipt among Black and White Adolescent Mothers: A Longitudinal Perspective." *Journal of Family Issues* 11:334–52.

Ruggles, Patricia. 1990. *Drawing the Line: Alternative Poverty Measures and Their Implications for Public Policy.* Washington, D.C.: Urban Institute Press.

Saluter, Arlene F. 1994. "Marital Status and Living Arrangements: March 1993." *Current Population Reports,* Series P20–478. Washington, D.C.: Bureau of the Census, Economics and Statistics Administration, U.S. Department of Commerce.

Sanger, Mary Bryna. 1983. "Household Structure among Welfare Families: Correlates and Consequences." *Journal of Marriage and the Family* 45:761–71.

South, Scott J. 1991. "Sociodemographic Differentials in Mate Selection Preferences." *Journal of Marriage and the Family* 53:928–40.

Spalter-Roth, Roberta M., and Heidi I. Hartmann. 1994a. "AFDC Recipients as Care-Givers and Workers: A Feminist Approach to Income Security Policy for American Women." *Social Politics: International Studies in Gender, State, and Society* 1:190–210.

————. 1994b. "Dependence on Men, the Market, or the State: The Rhetoric and Reality of Welfare Reform." *Journal of Applied Social Sciences* 18:55–70.

Spalter-Roth, Roberta M., Heidi I. Hartmann, and Linda M. Andrews. 1993. "Mothers, Children, and Low-Wage Work: The Ability to Earn a Family Wage." In *Sociology and the Public Agenda,* ed. William J. Wilson, 316–38. American Sociological Association Presidential Series. Newbury Park, Calif.: Sage.

Stack, Carol B. 1974. *All Our Kin: Strategies for Survival in a Black Community.* New York: Harper and Row.

Starr, Paul. 1986. "Health Care for the Poor: The Past Twenty Years." In *Fighting Poverty: What Works and What Doesn't,* ed. Sheldon H. Danziger and Daniel H. Weinberg, 106–32. Cambridge: Harvard University Press.

Sullivan, Mercer L. 1989. *"Getting Paid": Youth Crime and Work in the Inner City.* Anthropology of Contemporary Issues, ed. Roger Sanjek. Ithaca: Cornell University Press.

Survey Research Center. 1989. *A Panel Study of Income Dynamics: Procedures and Tape Codes (Documentation) 1987 Interviewing Year. Wave 20. A Supplement.* Vol. 1. Ann Arbor: Institute for Social Research, University of Michigan.

Teti, Douglas M., and Michael E. Lamb. 1989. "Socioeconomic and Marital Outcomes of Adolescent Marriage, Adolescent Childbirth, and Their Co-occurrence." *Journal of Marriage and the Family* 51:203–12.

Thornton, Arland, and Deborah S. Freedman. 1983. "The Changing American Family." *Population Bulletin* 38(4).

Tienda, Marta. 1990. "Welfare and Work in Chicago's Inner City." *American Economic Review* 80:372–76.

Tienda, Marta, and Haya Stier. 1991. "Joblessness and Shiftlessness: Labor Force Activity in Chicago's Inner City." In *The Urban Underclass,* ed. Christopher Jencks and Paul E. Peterson, 135–54. Washington, D.C.: Brookings Institution.

Trussell, T. James. 1976. "Economic Consequences of Teenage Childbearing." *Family Planning Perspectives* 8:184–90.

Trussell, T. James, and John Abowd. 1980. "Teenage Mothers, Labor Force Participation, and Wage Rates." *Canadian Studies in Population* 7:33–48.

Trussell, T. James, and Jane Menken. 1978. "Early Childbearing and Subsequent Fertility." *Family Planning Perspectives* 10:209–14, 216–18.

Tucker, M. Belinda. 1987. "The Black Male Shortage in Los Angeles." *Sociology and Social Research* 71:221–27.

Tuma, Nancy Brandon, and Michael T. Hannan. 1984. *Social Dynamics: Models and Methods.* Orlando: Academic Press.

Tuma, Nancy Brandon, Michael T. Hannan, and Lyle D. Groeneveld. 1979. "Dynamic Analysis of Event Histories." *American Journal of Sociology* 84:820–54.

Upchurch, Dawn M., and James F. McCarthy. 1990. "The Timing of a First Birth and High School Completion." *American Sociological Review* 55:224–34.

U.S. Bureau of the Census. 1995. "Income, Poverty, and Valuation of Noncash Benefits: 1993." *Current Population Reports,* Series P60–188. Washington, D.C.: Bureau of the Census, Economics and Statistics Administration, U.S. Department of Commerce.

U.S. Department of Labor, Bureau of Labor Statistics. 1981. *Employment and Earnings* 28(5).

———. 1983. *Employment and Earnings* 30(5).

———. 1985. *Employment and Earnings* 32(5).

———. 1987. *Employment and Earnings* 34(5).

———. 1989. *Employment and Earnings* 36(5).

U.S. Department of Labor, Employment and Training Administration. 1977. *Area Trends in Employment and Unemployment* (August–December). Washington, D.C.

———. 1979. *Area Trends in Employment and Unemployment* (July–December). Washington, D.C.

U.S. Department of Labor, Manpower Administration. 1969. *Area Trends in Employment and Unemployment* (July). Washington, D.C.

———. 1973. *Area Trends in Employment and Unemployment* (July). Washington, D.C.

———. 1975. *Area Trends in Employment and Unemployment* (May–July). Washington, D.C.

U.S. House of Representatives, Committee on Ways and Means. 1989. *General Explanation of the Family Support Act of 1988.* H.R. 1720, 100th Congress; Public Law 100–485. Washington, D.C.: U.S. Government Printing Office.

———. 1993. *1993 Green Book. Overview of Entitlement Programs.* Washington, D.C.: U.S. Government Printing Office.

———. 1994. *1994 Green Book. Overview of Entitlement Programs.* Washington, D.C.: U.S. Government Printing Office. CD-ROM.

U.S. National Center for Health Statistics, Division of Vital Statistics. 1967. *Vital Statistics of the United States 1965.* Vol. 1. *Natality.* Washington, D.C.: Public Health Service, U.S. Department of Health, Education, and Welfare.

Ventura, Stephanie J., Joyce A. Martin, Selma M. Taffell, T. J. Mathews, and Sally C. Clarke. 1995. "Advance Report of Final Natality Statistics, 1993." *Monthly Vital Statistics Report* 44(3, supplement).

Vinovskis, Maris A. 1988. *An "Epidemic" of Adolescent Pregnancy? Some Historical and Policy Considerations.* New York: Oxford University Press.

Wacquant, L. J. D., and William Julius Wilson. 1989. "Poverty, Joblessness, and the Social Transformation of the Inner City." In *Welfare Policy for the 1990s,* ed.

187

Phoebe H. Cottingham and David T. Ellwood, 70–102. Cambridge: Harvard University Press.

Wertheimer, Richard, and Kristin Anderson Moore. 1982. *Teenage Childbearing: Public Sector Costs*. Final Report. Washington, D.C.: Urban Institute.

Whitehead, Barbara Dafoe. 1993. "Dan Quayle Was Right." *Atlantic Monthly* 271:47–84.

Wilson, William Julius. 1987. *The Truly Disadvantaged: The Inner City, the Underclass, and Public Policy*. Chicago: University of Chicago Press.

———. 1991. "Studying Inner-City Social Dislocations: The Challenge of Public Agenda Research. 1990 Presidential Address." *American Sociological Review* 56:1–14.

Wiseman, Michael. 1977. "Change and Turnover in a Welfare Population." Berkeley: Institute of Business and Economic Research, University of California.

Yamaguchi, Kazuo. 1991. *Event History Analysis*. Newbury Park, Calif.: Sage Publications.

Zinn, Deborah K., and Rosemary C. Sarri. 1984. "Turning Back the Clock on Public Welfare." *Signs* 10:355–70.

Index

189

Index